Understanding Suffering in Schools

Drawing inspiration from Dr. Willi Schohaus's classic text *The Dark Places of Education*, this book contributes to the discussion by defining suffering in schools and providing a survey of the American school system's inadequacies in the early twenty-first century.

Through testimonies from former students on the ways they experienced suffering in school, this volume demonstrates how suffering can profoundly affect one's academic growth and development—or worse. By analyzing the findings within a multidisciplinary ethical and educational framework, this volume presents a moral vision for understanding the role that suffering plays in school.

Drawing on research in medicine, psychology, social sciences, religion, and education, this text weaves together many strands of thinking about suffering. This book is essential reading for academics, researchers, and postgraduate students in the fields of educational leadership, foundations of education, and those interested in both the history of education and critical contemporary accounts of schooling.

Joseph Polizzi is Associate Professor of Education and Educational Leadership at Sacred Heart University, USA.

William C. Frick is Professor of Educational Leadership and Policy Studies at the University of Oklahoma, USA.

Understanding Suffering in Schools

Shining a Light on the Dark Places of Education

Joseph Polizzi and William C. Frick

Routledge
Taylor & Francis Group

NEW YORK AND LONDON

First published 2023
by Routledge
605 Third Avenue, New York, NY 10158

and by Routledge
4 Park Square, Milton Park, Abingdon, Oxon, OX14 4RN

Routledge is an imprint of the Taylor & Francis Group, an informa business

Library of Congress Cataloging-in-Publication Data
A catalog record for this title has been requested

ISBN: 978-1-138-61091-0 (hbk)
ISBN: 978-1-032-32396-1 (pbk)
ISBN: 978-0-429-46549-9 (ebk)

DOI: 10.4324/9780429465499

Typeset in Bembo
by SPi Technologies India Pvt Ltd (Straive)

Dedicated to those
who have quietly suffered because of their school
experiences.

For all who seek to lead first from their heart.

In memory of
Stuart Manley Spangler, January 2, 1993–August 27,
2011

Contents

Illustrations

Figures

Tables

Acknowledgements

René Züst and the former students of Willi Schohaus who shared their notebooks and yearbooks from the Teacher Seminar at Kreuzlingen.
Schweizer Spiegel (October, November, December 1927) D 6155, Schweizerisches Sozialarchiv.
Geheeb Archives at the E'cole d'Humanite, Hasliberg, Switzerland, for providing information on the life of Willi Schohaus.
University of Reading, United Kingdom, Special Collections.
Sacred Heart University and Dean Michael Alfano for giving me a space to refine my thinking, teaching, and research in order to make a positive difference in the world. Colleagues Kristin Rainville and Jim Carl for their careful reading and editing during the latter stages of writing.
Sister Mary Persico, IHM, EdD, Marywood University President, for granting a sabbatical in the spring of 2018 in order to conduct research and begin writing.
The library staff at Sacred Heart University and Marywood University, particularly Mary Kay Maldonato.
Amy Paciej-Woodruff for assistance in the field.
Steven Jay Gross, Joan Shapiro, David P. Baker, Susan Laird, Brad Janey, May Spangler, Darcy Ronan, René Roselle, Mark Murphy, Marc Brasof, Anthony Sarchiapone, Pete Ippolito, and Kendrick Norris for their wise counsel, encouragement and support along the way.
Francesco Mulé, MD, for his knowledge of palliative care and insight into the human heart.
To our graduate students for their understanding, gracefulness, and dedication to the careful and difficult social, emotional, and academic work of teaching and leading. A particularly loud shout goes out to Joe's former high school students from Cobble Hill School of American Studies in Brooklyn, NY.—You make me proud!
Daria Corey, Jess Beardsworth, and Sarah Bergers for their unwavering administrative support during turbulent times.
Lee Sebastiani and her exceptional editing and unique ability to roll with it all.
Matt Friberg, Elsbeth Wright, Alice Salt, and AnnaMary Goodall at Taylor Francis/Routledge.

To all those who placed their trust in us by agreeing to talk and whom we cannot name: respecting their privacy requires preserving their anonymity.

Bill's Covid pandemic/endemic period of grace that permitted time and space for reflecting and writing.

Finally, Joe's deepest gratitude is reserved for his family—Éva, Lily Julia, and Sofie Joy whose love, patience, and laughter fuel his dedication—Sétálunk sétálunk egy kis dombra lecsücsülünk csüccs. Csókolom.

Foreword

Susan C. Faircloth PhD
(Coharie)
Colorado State University

"Searching for Hope and Purpose in the Midst of Suffering"

"...the need to tell our stories remains the powerful imperative of a powerful form of resistance"

(Smith, 1999, p. 35).

I am honored to have been asked to write the foreword for *Understanding Suffering in Schools: Shining a Light on the Dark Places of Education* authored by Joseph Polizzi (Sacred Heart University) and William Frick (University of Oklahoma). I had the great fortune of meeting Polizzi and Frick during their doctoral studies at the Pennsylvania State University, where they worked closely with Drs. Paul Begley and Jackie Stefkovich, two of the foundational scholars in the field of ethics in education. I'm quite certain the way in which Polizzi and Frick approach the framing and writing of this book is shaped, in large part, by their courses and conversations with Begley and Stefkovich. Their legacies live on in those they taught, mentored, and more importantly, befriended.

This book is written at a time when the world seems engulfed in pain, loss, and suffering—fraught with uncertainty and chaos. Unfortunately, schools have not been exempt. Educators and students, alike, have been dealt the difficult task of teaching and learning in the midst of chaos. This has led many educators to question their purpose and their why. Simultaneously, students have been forced to adjust to learning in physical isolation, in spaces that place them at increased risk for illness and sometimes, even death, or a combination of the two. Yet, in the midst of these challenging times, learning and caring have not ceased. What we've witnessed is the ultimate moral and ethical dilemma for those who teach and learn.

The gravity of the conditions in which we are living and learning today underscore the importance and urgency of the questions Polizzi and Frick attempt to answer in this book:

1. From what did students suffer most in school?
2. What are the experiential characteristics and effects of that suffering?
3. How can school suffering accounts be interpreted considering existing literature...?
4. How do the categories of suffering from Schohaus (1927) compare with themes of suffering in schools today?"

While these are critically important questions, what was most powerful to me was the explicit questioning and ultimately the naming and categorization of suffering experienced in schools. Throughout nearly 80 interviews, Polizzi and Frick heard stories of:

1. "affront[s] to personhood-injury to dignity",
2. "anxiety, stress and fear",
3. lack of "companionship and isolation",
4. issues related to "personal, cultural, and social identity",
5. "lateral violence" in the form of harassment, discrimination and bullying,
6. "educator indiscretion, impropriety and transgression",
7. "corporeal disaffection-physicality" or not being accepted due to bodily traits or characteristics,
8. "struggles with learning", and
9. incidents of "solicitude" where parents and family members suffered when they saw the children and youth they cared for hurting.

Naming these acts of suffering required incredible vulnerability and courage on the part of the study's participants. In doing so, they helped to give voice to what many have endured but have not had the agency or opportunity to express out loud. Unfortunately, as Lorde (1977) so aptly reminds us, "...silence will not protect..." (p. 41) those who suffer. Thus, it is critically important that these stories be heard and honored.

However, naming these hurts is only the first step. Real healing and change require educators and school leaders to acknowledge and own both our complicity in enabling suffering to seed and grow within our schools and our role in "...alleviat[ing] ... suffering brought about by people, policies, and practices..." (Polizzi & Frick). But it does not stop there. Polizzi and Frick also issue a call to action for education scholars, to interrogate the ways in which our scholarly work can help to transform schools into more caring and safe spaces, or at minimum, places in which suffering can be experienced as productive—something to be learned from—rather than destructive—something that destroys those who suffer.

Although Polizzi and Frick's study is limited in size and scope, the themes that emerge resonate with my own experiences as an American Indian woman, mother, and scholar. As I read their work, I was reminded of my own educative experience and the ways in which this experience has shaped how I parent, teach, lead, and research today. As a parent, I send my child to school each morning with the hope that the school will see her for the beautiful, bright, humorous, being that she is. Then, I close the door and fear that they will not. This fear persists until I see her safely return home in the afternoon. Only then can I exhale. As a teacher, I hope that the lessons I share will lead to more culturally affirming learning spaces, yet. As a scholar, I hope that my words will transcend the academy and resonate with those doing the heart work in schools and classrooms. Yet, I fear that my lessons and my words will not affect the change I seek. Still, I hope. (And, I sense that Polizzi and Frick do too.)

I hope for those around the world, for whom schools have served as both sites of refuge and resistance and tools of pain and suffering. I hope for those from historically marginalized groups for whom schools have not served as sites of possibility and promise but rather as vehicles of acculturation and assimilation. I write these words not as an indictment of those who work in schools, but in hope and solidarity with those who suffer in silence. I write these words for those who care so deeply for their students, who know that schools can and should be safe harbors for those who are deemed most vulnerable; for those who approach this work with a deep and abiding ethic of care and responsibility and a moral compass that compels them to do right, to teach right, to lead and learn with purpose and compassion.

While engaging with the work of Polizzi and Frick helped me to better understand suffering within the context of schools, they also fueled a sense of urgency to move beyond suffering; to effect real, meaningful, and lasting change in school; to support children and youth in finding and exercising their own agency and voice; and to listen to and honor what these children and youth are telling us. As my own child shared, "children are smart Mom. You should listen to us."

Polizzi and Frick also remind us that "student suffering" does not occur in isolation. Teachers and school leaders are also suffering—suffering because of the educational practices they are compelled to implement; suffering because they lack fiscal and human resources to do what needs to be done within their schools; suffering because larger societal and political systems fail to view educators as professionals worthy of compensation or respect; suffering because they are tired, sick, and scared; suffering in silence, afraid that speaking out will only increase their suffering; suffering in place because they can't bear to leave; suffering on the outside because they can no longer bear to stay. Parents and family members are suffering too—suffering because they see their children suffering and they can't make it stop.

But, in the midst of all this suffering, Polizzi and Frick also offer a sliver of hope; hope that we can find pockets of possibility and joy within our schools and that students and educators, alike, can rediscover purpose, meaning, and joy, even in the midst of suffering.

For now, we must continue to ask:

How do we make sense of what's happening in schools? to schools?

How do we support educators in teaching and leading effectively in the midst of pain and suffering?

How do we heal the minds, bodies, hearts, and spirits that have been harmed by schools?

How do we lessen suffering in schools?

How?

Refusing to ask these questions is to fail our students and our schools.

In Peace, Solidarity, and Joy,

Susan

References

Lorde, A. (1977, December 28). The transformation of silence into language and action. Paper delivered at the Modern Language Association's "Lesbian and Literature Panel." Chicago, Illinois.

Smith, L. T. (1999). *Decolonizing methodologies: Research and Indigenous peoples* (1st ed.). Zed Books/University of Otago Press.

Preface

In this book we highlight the work of Swiss educator Willi Schohaus (1897–1981). Our title *Understanding Suffering in Schools: Shining a Light on the Dark Places of Education* makes a mirrored reference to Schohaus's (1932/2012) *The Dark Places of Education: With a Collection of Seventy-Eight Reports of School Experiences*, where the original responses to the question, "From what did you suffer most in school?" are reported and discussed. Our method was to reflect and honor the spirit of Schohaus's study today: 90 years since first publication of *Dark Places*.

We bring your attention to his work because we believe Schohaus provides a solemn yet spirited vision into the twenty-first century for schools and those who inhabit them. He was a progressive educator who fostered a student-centered, less regimented yet still disciplined classroom environment where self-governance pervaded and a more casual, informal social relationship between the teacher and students was enacted. His ideal school culture married hard work, camaraderie, sincerity, academics, and time for leisure that influenced his students for years to come. All practice ideal of what we believe is needed in schools today.

One might be convinced that a study of suffering in schools is to be focused on sadness, lament, and despair, and although there is that in this book, we came to learn through our interviews, and reflecting on Schohaus's work, that helping a student struggling through suffering demands humility, empathy, and grace. These are virtues needing more attention for our schools in our post-pandemic lives with students ... and also with each other.

We believe Schohaus was drawn to the question of suffering in schools for the same reason we are; because witnessing the results of pernicious good intentions of school policies, practices, and people and not being able to bear the detrimental impact they have on the lives of students. Schohaus's ethic, and one to which we subscribe to as well, centers on the teacher–student relationship as paramount and is founded on a mutual human and social commitment. Because "suffering constantly accompanies human striving" (Goldberg, 2001, p. 13), studying suffering within the context of schools is necessary for understanding the often difficult emotions involved with learning. In this way, we are better positioned to see how suffering in school lives in juxtaposition to happiness and joy.

xvi   *Preface*

This study of suffering in schools leads us to confirm and advocate for what Schohaus notes, that "happiness is compatible with the deepest ethical seriousness, and indeed cannot be imagined without it. The right kind of goodness provides the warmth of a flourishing educational climate, and happiness its light" (Schohaus, 1932/2012, p. 82).

Reference

Goldberg, C. (2001). Concerning madness and human suffering, *Pastoral Psychology*, *50*(1) 13–23.

Schohaus, W. (1932/2012). *The dark places of education* (M. Chadwick, Trans.) Routledge. (Original work published 1930).

1 Contributions to Suffering Based on Critical Contemporary Accounts of Schooling

Introduction

On the surface, suffering does not present itself as a very pleasant or edifying point of inquiry about schools. Nevertheless, defining suffering through the experiences and points of view of students provides us with an intimate survey of the contemporary inadequacies of U.S. schooling (deficiencies that we posit are universal ones that are just as prevalent in school systems around the world). The dark places in education, according to those schooled, are the lived experiences of students succumbing to or overcoming a range of circumstances that can be characterized as suffering. Both overt and hidden suffering through the course of education is a problem as old as schooling itself (Schohaus, 2012/1932). And, exposing that suffering is necessary, now more than ever, so that our collective understanding and empathy can increasingly lead to more robustly responsive schools that create the conditions for all students to holistically thrive.

Suffering of course is not limited to schooling, and we certainly recognize that. There are limits to what schools can achieve in effectively responding to the myriad sources where suffering may originate. There are many factors that influence the lives of youth. In this book, we are concerned about the contribution of schooling in the experience of suffering and how schools could be made better by our analysis.

In the following excerpt, we can listen to the voice of a student, now long graduated, recalling a particular moment when he was left alone and wanting:

> For one reason or another no one would really want to talk with me or hang out with me. I specifically remember fourth grade birthday [planning]. The teacher said, "Arlo, you can have your birthday celebration during recess." I remember being very excited because I wasn't allowed to have sweets at home. I convinced my parents and I could bring them because we're celebrating. I just wanted to have fun and enjoy it. The teacher said, "OK, well it's Arlo's birthday today, so let's celebrate" and then recess happened and everybody just left. It was just me and the teacher sitting in the classroom. And I felt like I was an outcast [thinking], "Oh well, nobody really does care." It was tough. Throughout school it was just trying not

DOI: 10.4324/9780429465499-1

> to be noticed, and I did a lot of trying to forget. I became an isolationist. I would go off to and do my own thing. I was happier not around people and learned how to build up a protective barrier.

From an early age, this child encountered shame, social separation, and stigma in a place where, at its most fundamental and elementary levels, students ought to feel they are an equal and accepted member of a community where they can develop pride and acceptance among peers. Unfortunately, this was not Arlo's experience.

Our interest in researching and writing about suffering in schools stems from a feeling of being called to those who hurt. Early professional experiences working with elementary and high school children from challenging circumstances of poverty, neglect, and disability have framed our entire trajectory of learning and personal expiation. Later, in our studies toward the terminal degree, we noticed that with the passage of the No Child Left Behind Act of 2001, P.L. 107-110, 20 U.S.C. § 6319 (2002) the federal government began "holding school leaders' feet to the fire" to gain compliance with the aims and goals of the new law. Stakes became higher, and punishment for refusing or resisting to follow along was real and palpable. The culture of schooling changed. Two years after the tragedy of Columbine, rather than moving in the direction of a kinder, gentler approach, a turn toward more draconian policies, educationally and socially, in schools, has become more prevalent. Furthermore, the post-pandemic world has, in many ways, fostered a profound culture of suffering in schools. Working with vulnerable students requires compassion and humility, but it also requires something more, and that something more is what we sought to discover through this study.

Although there are extraordinary educators, schools, and organizational systems expressing deep purpose and focused enterprise dedicated to a positively formative experience for each child, there is, unfortunately, considerable hurt, waste, and even more regrettable, detriment and harm. We aim to harness the feelings, perspectives, and afflictions that come with the suffering which fuels the passion for the work we do. Intimately, as parents, and as engaged community members, we see and are sensitized to this suffering as we both equally struggle with others in turning perhaps an (un)welcome critical lens on the work of schools.

We acknowledge that some may feel strongly that a study of suffering requires alluding to religious discussions, yet, public school settings hold little tolerance for notions of spirituality and even an existential curricular perspective has become taboo in professional environments. Nevertheless, we maintain a humanist viewpoint. According to the American Humanist Association, "Being without theism or other supernatural beliefs, affirms our ability and responsibility to lead ethical lives of personal fulfilment that aspire to the greater good" (American Humanist Association, 2021). In our view, this position is a practical and palatable approach for school workers who are striving toward educational and community leadership. Of course, a robust spiritual life nurtures the necessary seeds of wellness that ultimately only serve professional growth and discernment necessary for this important work, and we address religious perspectives on suffering later in the book. Yet, it is in the clear exhibition of resilience and courage, grace, compassion, and humility enacted and embodied by all forms of leadership in the public sphere that will aid the suffering student.

Our working definition of suffering in schools is an affliction of the mind, body, heart or spirit, or some combination of these elements. It means to undergo, experience or endure, or be subjected to something harmful or painful which is inflicted or imposed on one intentionally or unintentionally in a school context. Suffering in school is often the outcome of pernicious good intentions on the part of the people, policies and daily practices in a school setting. In our leadership vision, though, suffering in schools, and the call for com-passion are forever entwined. The Latin word for suffering is *passionis*:

> This power of com-passion is what moves a person to engage him- or herself in concrete ways towards the alleviation of the world's suffering. It guides us in making concrete decisions to take on the real and difficult tasks in our actual situation.
>
> (Habito, 2004, p. 109)

Many educators lead with a caring passion. We believe this study can help teachers, principals, and school superintendents understand their students better and find grace in their own disposition to go beyond a professional courtesy in meeting the needs of struggling students. In many ways, our collective compassion is working inspiration as we strive to listen better to the desperate, but all too common, call of struggle. In the excerpt below, we listen to the voice of a woman, now in her 30s, looking back on a formative experience she had in school that forever changed her life.

> As a child, school didn't come easy to me. I had to study hard to even just pass. I needed a lot of reviewing which wasn't always allowed and at times it was embarrassing. As I got older, I was able to find different strategies to help keep up and get better grades. Today, my son has this same problem, and has been diagnosed with ADHD. It has been a huge struggle for him to keep up. It breaks my heart hearing him suffer through the same things I did. My darkest moment in school isn't really mine, but something I witnessed happen to someone else in school. In my junior high school, we shared extracurricular classes, such as art and music, with special needs kids. I remember one time in my art class, there was a special needs boy who must have been having a bad day, or a particularly hard time with this art project. He was very upset and was making "weird" noises and gestures. Some kids were getting annoyed by this. One decided to start yelling at the boy. They were complaining and didn't know why we needed to share classes with "retards" anyway. They were all being extremely mean. That only made things worse and the special needs boy got louder and more frustrated. Eventually they had to take him out of the classroom to calm him down. I remember feeling so bad for the boy. I know he must have

understood even a little bit of what the other person was saying about him and to him. And other kids who were more verbal but still special needs definitely understood. It broke my heart. And for what? The disrespectful kid didn't even get in trouble. The teacher just reprimanded them and said it was wrong.

She found her own challenges, but was able to overcome them. Her son struggles with the same problems she overcame, and she can help him. In the incident she observed, a bully was not disciplined by the teacher for hurtful words and actions to another student in the class. No consequences were felt, no sense of camaraderie or protocols were established in the classroom for students to help others less fortunate in talent. The lack of an accepting and tolerant community, and poor disciplinary practice set out by the teacher, subsequently inspired this young woman to go on and become a special education teacher herself.

At an alternative school in New York City, we learned how students from diverse backgrounds found a home in a non-traditional school after they were discriminated against and bullied and hurt in the traditional school system. In this school, teachers and administrators embodied a professional, compassionate disposition and a caring, empathetic approach that was tied to a personalized curriculum, created by the teachers themselves. Textbooks were secondary and a human touch took precedent and was evident throughout the building. Classroom lessons and the school's methods were met through an understanding of the myriad complexities students bring to and face in their lives, not just in school, but outside of school as unique creatures in this world. Perhaps this school was a rarity, perhaps not. It was successful because of the cultural protocols and the attitudes and expertise of the compassionate professionals at work there. In other schools we saw practices, organizational cultures and contexts, inane and inhumane policies and careless, compliant persons who exacerbated suffering in ways that showcased the pernicious good intentions of the rules and regulations governing the work of educators. We listened to parents whose beloved children had faced trials in school, suffering because of the dispositions of teachers who lacked the qualities of patience and empathy and administrators who capitulated to a uniform, often uninformed, and outdated professional ethic.

From the potency of our own lived experiences, and the experiences of those we interviewed, the epistemological position and thesis of the text are that people suffer throughout their lives because of events, incidents, and experiences they had while in school that have gone unresolved. These experiences either aided in defining a person's life in a robust and resilient fashion that contributed to their eventual well-being or hindered their overall growth and development over the long term. The suffering/well-being connection is that experiences during schooling are catalysts for one's basic survival and resiliency that eventually contribute to well-being beyond school later in life.

The Swiss educator Willi Schohaus, whom we will discuss at length in the following chapter, has been a kindred spirit for us throughout the writing of this book. In his text *The Dark Places of Education* (2012/1932) he attempted to

answer the question, "What is wrong with our schools?" by asking his participants, "From what did you suffer most in school?" Today, clearly, this question is
on the minds of many people, yet, it strikes a harsh tone, which is not our aim.
His question though is straightforward and is worth reflecting on for more than
a brief moment. Following Schohaus's lead over a century ago, we are interested
in a subtle and less frequently asked question: *What contributes to suffering based on
critical, contemporary accounts of schooling?* And, as we conclude later in the text, a
reflection on the question of *How (and why?) does school as an institution denigrate?*
With this question in mind, we will discuss approaches to school leadership that
can alleviate unproductive suffering brought about by people, policies, and practices in the schooling context.

Overall, this monograph is the presentation of research conducted on the
social influences impacting schools that cause and create a context where suffering inhabits and inhibits the setting. Finally, we will attempt to address thoughtful ways to ensure more flourishing experiences for students. With this said, the
purposes of this study are as follows:

- Inform the work of school sector professionals through narratives of suffering in school.
- Highlight the work of the Swiss educator Dr. Willi Schohaus [1897–1981]
  who asked his original research question, "From what do you suffer most in
  school?" and bring this inquiry into the 21st century.
- Present a moral vision for understanding the role suffering plays in school.
- Contribute to a body of knowledge that can be used to better understand
  and alleviate suffering and increase well-being in school settings.
- Address Schohaus's findings from the early 20th century and ours in the
  early 21st century.

Situating Suffering in School Life

Throughout history, suffering has played a role in learning, schooling, and more
broadly, education, and suffering contributes positively to or detracts from a
person's well-being over time. The idea, question, and experiences of suffering
are crucial for all people. No one can avoid or escape it, and it is decisive for the
meaning we give to our lives as well as our actions (Pinckaers, 2015). Particularly
in a school setting, suffering poses existential problems of identity and continuity of self (Charmaz, 1999), and, in doing so, poses unique challenges to
students, teachers, and leaders. The act of discerning, understanding, alleviating,
and overcoming suffering is a significant human activity that motivates as well as
contributes to an ideation of success that necessitates physical, mental, spiritual,
emotional, and social aspects of personhood; yet, succumbing to suffering can
have long-lasting negative effects. It is a "deep and complex phenomenon intimately and intricately related to the very nature of human existence" (Taylor &
Watson, 1989, p. 1). Suffering may be understood as something of value which
makes possible spiritual connection and transformation (Norris, 2009 as cited

in Fitzpatrick et al., 2016). Human suffering has inspired some of the world's significant accomplishments in many fields such as art, music, literature, and science, but we also may never know what great accomplishments might have been due to an individual's yielding to the challenges they faced in their lives. There is also a subtext of individualism at work, atomistic or otherwise, embedded in Western thought, education, and culture, that works to negate the importance of social cohesion, group identity, and community in overcoming and alleviating suffering (Heuser, 2005). By involving ourselves as school leaders in the difficulty of understanding what suffering is in human existence, particularly in schools at an individual and group level, we may arrive at a better position from which to appreciate what suffering means and does to people (Wilkinson, 2005). As Mintz (2012, p. 249) noted, "The widely held progressive belief that learning should be pleasurable and painless denies the significance of frustration, confusion, distress and other painful moments in learning that ultimately inhibit growth". Aeschylus wrote in the Greek tragedy *The Agamemnon*:

> Tis Zeus alone who shows the perfect way
> Of Knowledge: He hath ruled,
> Men shall learn wisdom, by affliction schooled.
> In visions of night, like dropping rain,
> Descend the many memories of pain
> Before the spirit's sight: through tears and dole
> Comes wisdom o'er the unwilling sole.
> (458 BCE/1961/)

On the one hand, we have to acknowledge, as many teachers and administrators do, that the presence of affliction as a means of schooling is part of the hardship of learning and study. Nevertheless, and conversely, Thomas Aquinas asserted that suffering diminishes the faculty of learning and can even take it away entirely when it is intense. Reasonable sadness, a grounded, minimal emotional response, can have a positive impact on learning and self-discipline (Pinckaers, 2015). This is clearly illustrated by the necessary, earnest, at times even somber, emotional, and physical state that proves necessary in disciplining oneself to sit in a study carrel for hours on end preparing for an exam or withstanding the other means we use to face our other academic or personal challenges. Suffering in school, *because of school*, can either "lead to development or diminishment; a path to finding resolution or gaining wisdom or a route to sinking into depression and slipping into despair" (Charmaz, 1999, p. 366). This despair, in varying degrees, can afflict a person for a lifetime. Davies asserted:

> Suffering signifies that all is not as it should be, and that something [potentially] harmful is impending our way. Suffering signifies that certain social or psychological conditions are holding us back and is therefore the first step towards liberation from subjugation and towards development of the self. Suffering is the incentive par excellence to make us reform our situation.
> (2012, p. 37)

So, we can appreciate the two-sided coin of suffering, particularly when it comes to the experience of schooling. And with this appreciation come more questions and the raison d'etre for our study. Arguably, for us, "the moral and intellectual tensions borne under the attempt to acknowledge and make known what suffering does to people hold the potential to be highly productive for the acquisition of social understanding" (Wilkinson & Kleinman, 2016, p. 83). And we would include with Wilkinson and Kleinman's (2016) assertion the potential of deriving moral insight for creating the conditions for all students' flourishing.

Part of this social understanding and moral insight is manifest in relational practice where empathy plays a part. The ability to see, become aware, seek understanding, empathize, and show compassion—a heightened prosocial praxis toward students—is a disposition necessary toward alleviating suffering in schools and promoting a healthy school culture. This study serves to highlight the implications brought forth for a comprehensive professional disposition that ensures not only academic study, but the mental-health and well-being of students and members of an entire school community. We believe the disposition can develop and grow exponentially as a function of moral school leadership. Saturn (2017) found that "studies of moral elevation have shown that merely witnessing compassion prompts an array of changes to one's physiology and psychological state and inspires others to perform compassionate acts in turn" (p. 128). This implores the educational leader's sensate understanding of moral elevation and their ethical responsibility to role model as an orienting compassionate caregiver in the school setting.

Some Contemporary Causes of Suffering in School

What comparative internationalists call the "education revolution" has caused unprecedented growth in the number of people going to school throughout the world (Baker, 2014). With the hegemony of the global education reform movement, or GERM, a term Sahlberg (2012) coined now firmly in place, mass schooling with its pervasive global culture has left a broadly humane, holistic commitment to children as a minor subtext. The key characteristics of GERM are clearly observable: the calibration of education across local, state, and national boundaries; a predominant focus on core subjects that degrade the value of arts; a continued search for low-risk ways to reach learning goals through the use of cookie-cutter curriculums, or preplanned lessons; the use of corporate-style management models in educational leadership and heavily data-driven techniques as a driver of school improvement; and all of this buttressed by standardized achievement testing and accountability mandates.

Additionally, we see the continued belief that test score-based measures of school quality are controlling parents' perceptions of educational excellence, whereas school quality along this dimension is not strongly associated with pupil happiness and enjoyment of the learning environment (Gibbons & Silva, 2008). With technocratic schooling it becomes increasingly clear that teacher agency, autonomy, and professionalism are continuously under attack (Anderson &

Cohen, 2015). The prevalence of bullying and cyberbullying and the effects of social media highlight children mistreating each other and being mistreated by adult caregivers (Nesi & Prinstein, 2015; Hase et al., 2015; Vachon et al., 2015). The shocking ethical and moral infractions on the part of teachers and school personnel have become a regular part of our daily news (Shapiro and Stefkovich, 2016; Balzer & Frick, 2017). Although not legal in every state or country, the continued legitimacy of corporal punishment and the ethos it perpetrates is more than troubling (Maiti, 2021; Crain, 2016). The marked increase in violence, terror, and carnage in schools and on school-aged children, including Uvalde, TX, Columbine, CO; Sandy Hook, CT; Lancaster, PA; Luther, OK; and Parkland, FL in the United States, shocks the conscience. The limits of the one-dimensional, post-pandemic schooling model dependent on video conferencing have diminished the social and emotional needs of kids and teens and have prompted ever-increasing mental health, anxiety, and stress disorders raising serious concerns for school district leaders, teachers, parents, students, and communities (Adelman & Taylor, 2021) (Figure 1.1).

Pre-pandemic, the number of superintendents who indicated that improving student mental health services was a priority for their schools jumped from 35% in 2016 to 52% in 2018. Moreover, as of November 2021, based on responses from 359 U.S. school superintendents, the top three concerns were the mental health of their students, teachers and principals (Diliberti & Schwartz, 2022) 45% of superintendents cited "capacity to assist students with non-academic needs, including health and mental health," as a significant problem for their schools

Figure 1.1 Student protestors from March for Our Lives. Photograph by Jeffrey Seymour.

(New York State Council of School Superintendents, 2018).. In one instant response, the State of Connecticut passed legislation allowing students two mental health wellness days in a school year allowing for a student to attends to their emotional and psychological well-being in lieu of attending school (An Act Concerning Social Equity and the Health Safety and Education of Children, Public Act 21-462021).

Sadly, in the United States, suicide rates and attempts by school students, particularly among girls between the ages of 10 and 14, have risen (Bichell, 2016). The suicide rate among boys aged 15 to 19 increased by nearly a third between 2007 and 2015, and the suicide rate among girls the same age more than doubled in that time frame (Vestal, 2018). The state of Florida Youth Risk Behaviour Survey documents in 2017: 28% of Florida high school students reported feeling sad or hopeless for two or more weeks in a row; 14% reported purposely hurting themselves without wanting to die; 14% reported having seriously considered attempting suicide; 11% reported having made a plan to commit suicide; and 8% reported a suicide attempt (Florida State Board of Education, 2019). The Higher Education Research Institute (HERI) at UCLA found that in 2016 approximately 11.9% of incoming college freshman report feeling depressed frequently. It was in 1985 that HERI began asking incoming freshman "if they felt overwhelmed by all I had to do" during the previous year. In 1985, 18% said they did, in 2010 that number increased to 29%, and in 2016 it rose to 41% (Denizet-Lewis, 2017). In the National Student Affairs Professional Association annual census, student mental health was ranked the number one issue by 750 chief student affairs officers at both public and private, two-year and four-year institutions. What is not resolved, or may actually have occurred in earlier schooling, moves up to the next stages of a student's education.

Educators in the United States are not alone in dealing with issues of stress, anxiety and depression, and other mental health issues that cause student suffering. As just one international example, in India, suicide among students is a serious, significant, and growing concern. Data from the Ministry of Home Affairs in India show that across states and territories in India, suicide rates among students are on the rise. In 2014, there were 8,068 suicides, in 2015 there were 8,934, and in 2016 there were 9,474 students who took their own lives, of which 2,413 were attributed to "failure in examinations" (Kundu, 2018). Furthermore, according to the latest estimates from the World Health Organization, more than 300 million people are now living with depression, an increase of more than 18% between 2005 and 2015 (World Health Organization [WHO], 2017). There is no doubt that students, teachers, support staff, administrators, and others who work with children are included in this statistic contributing to the context in schools where the causes of suffering breed.

Engagement, Well-Being, and Happiness

These facts and disturbing developments have deleteriously affected and influenced the lives of many students, families, and communities. For one, creating a culture where students are engaged and motivated to learn is an age-old problem, with modern concerns and distractions in its way. The UCLA School Mental Health Project asked, "To what degree is student engagement a problem?" They found that in urban and rural schools serving economically disadvantaged families, teachers said they are lucky if 10 to 15% of their students come to class ready to engage with the lessons; in suburban areas, the percentage reported of students ready is at 75% (Fredricks et al., 2019). There is an urgent and ever-increasing need for an [educational] approach that will be able to reach a majority of young people and be of a preventative, inspirational, and educational, rather than a remedial, nature (Popovic, 2013). In a hopeful, informed, and undeniably urgent move, in the summer of 2018 the Government of India along with his holiness the Dalai Lama introduced a "happiness curriculum" to address the growing student concerns in India. The curriculum includes meditation, joyful exercises, indoor games, storytelling, group discussions, skits, individual and group presentations, and activities for rapport building and teamwork (Kundu, 2018). In the United States, Social and Emotional Learning (SEL) and Social Emotional and Academic Learning (SEAL) have found a place in the lexicon of educational policy and practice as have trauma-informed and healing-centered educational approaches (Ginwright, 2018). SEL includes multifaceted lessons in self-awareness, self-management, responsible decision-making, and the ability to learn about and manage emotions and interactions in ways that benefit the self and others, helping children and youth succeed in schooling, the workplace, relationships, and citizenship. SEL programs intentionally cultivate a caring, participatory, and equitable learning environment with evidence-based practices that actively involve all students in their social, emotional, and academic growth (CASEL, 2019). As an outgrowth of trauma-informed schools, as Ginwright (2018) noted, a healing-centered approach recognizes that the sufferer is more than the pain they have experienced, and

> offers an important departure from solely viewing young people through the lens of harm and focuses on asset-driven strategies that highlight possibilities for well-being. An asset driven strategy acknowledges that young people are much more than the worst thing that happened to them, and builds upon their experiences, knowledge, skills and curiosity as positive traits to be enhanced.
>
> (p. 4)

New York State, Virginia, and Florida in the United States have all passed laws requiring the teaching of mental health lessons at the elementary, middle and high school levels beginning in the 2018 school year. In July of 2018, New York introduced its comprehensive guide to Mental Health Education Literacy in Schools: *Linking to a Continuum of Well-Being* that introduces key mental health and well-being benchmarks for a positive school climate and culture (NYSED, 2018). According to Eades et al. (2014), classroom happiness extends beyond feeling good to feeling competent, challenged, autonomous, respected, and involved in meaningful activities. These issues helped to frame this inquiry by highlighting student narratives pertaining to school conditions, cultures, and contexts, about the impact and subsequent alleviation of suffering on the social and emotional lives and well-being of students, teachers, and school communities as a whole. Our present and ongoing concern, particularly in light of the 2020 pandemic, is that the initiatives to address the growing social and emotional needs of students who are suffering are not simply given lip service and inevitably lost within the language of academic standards, achievement testing, and competition at all and any costs. At the same time, we also advocate for considering how we look at students and our inclination to pathologize their challenging experiences, rather than understand the school conditions that may very well have contributed to them.

Terminology of Suffering and Well-Being

How suffering is linked to mental health and student well-being is a vital part of this study. Davies (2012) noted two types of psychological suffering: *unproductive* and *productive*. Unproductive suffering is a passive state governed by feelings, thoughts, and habits that are destructive to our quality of life, but we do nothing to eradicate the roots of these feelings, thoughts, and habits; whereas productive suffering is an emotional experience we undergo while actively moving forward from a negative state to a positive one. For our well-being, Davies continued, we must endure the suffering entailed in overcoming the barriers to our development that prevent us from advancing further. Discerning between these sufferings and their distinctive outcomes can be a complicated matter, especially when observing affliction as it occurs. Our study entertains this distinction of suffering while highlighting its unproductive dimension as it implicates children's well-being.

Corradi-Fiumara (2015) has called these same phenomena *uncreative* and *creative suffering*, declaring that our greatest need is the capacity to use our very own suffering in a fruitful way. The capacity to handle pain creatively is essential. Corradi-Fiumara continued that an understanding of suffering does not need to be damaging or pointless, but we are reminded that it is often critical to a person's emancipation. It is the lessons our suffering can teach us, and putting those teachings into action that can be achieved by facing, experiencing, and learning from our own suffering whenever it may occur (Davies, 2012). Encountering a helping and caring professional in a time of need, in a school setting, Davies and Corradi-Fiumara's ideas become relevant to our understanding of how suffering can be framed and lay the groundwork for its alleviation. Furthermore, useless and dangerous suffering, resulting from the pernicious good intentions of schooling, oppression, punishment, and coercion, is imposed arbitrarily and artificially upon children, causing them pain while they neither learn nor become tolerant (Mintz, 2012). We will see later in the book that all these types of suffering exist in school settings.

Well-being is a dynamic state that is enhanced when people can fulfill their personal and social goals and achieve a sense of purpose in a school setting and in society (Stratham & Chase, 2010). Stable well-being is when individuals have the psychological, social, emotional, and physical resources they need to meet a particular psychological, social, and/or physical challenge (Dodge et al., 2012). One way to determine well-being is by how a person interacts with the world in different stages of their life. Well-being requires a healthy disposition of caring for oneself differently through each stage. Learning how to do so is not necessarily automatic. As Frick (2011) explained, at the high school level in particular, schools proclaim, instill, and require a mandate for students to take care of themselves within an environment that claims to look out for the best interests of all students; yet these same school environments leave many students in questionable emotional states and troubled circumstances.

Suffering and Student Voice

In the organizational realm, student voice initiatives have revealed and addressed cultural and structural issues hampering teaching and learning, resulting in socially just institutions. At the organizational level, student voice initiatives have uncovered and tackled cultural and structural issues undermining teaching and learning, making schools more effective, and socially just (Brasof, 2015). As a corollary, communication is key to identifying and handling suffering, which is why a first step in alleviating suffering is finding/giving voice to one's lament (Younger, 1995). Sharon Todd (2002) put it this way:

> Listening to stories of suffering can be difficult, painful, even traumatic. Yet listen we do and listen we must. If we do not bear witness to these stories, then we are rendered incapable of responding, of answering for our or others' actions, of taking a position of responsibility.
>
> (p. 405)

The act of recounting suffering in the face of disruption ensures continuity and wholeness (Charmaz, 1999). Allowing the space for listening to and understanding how students have suffered in schools will offer insight—insight into approaches to fostering social, emotional, and academic well-being as an aim of effective pedagogy, graceful dispositions toward students, programming, and leadership ethics. A sixth intuitive sense is particularly necessary when encountering suffering in someone else. Often, as Frank (2001) noted, it is precisely because someone is suffering that they cannot speak of their suffering. A suffering student is not inclined to speak of what is afflicting them because they fear "their words could never convey what they felt but would reduce those feelings to complaints and specific concerns" (p. 354). This work of discerning and understanding and alleviating suffering in a school setting requires sensibilities that are subtle, caring, sensitive, empathetic, even existential in nature and counterintuitive at times to professional expectations, norms, and ethics. For instance, believing that community building in schools is a political and humanistic-spiritual activity, the collective blending of personal narratives by willingly choosing the premise that our lives are fundamentally interrelated, places practitioners in profound roles as healing agents (Frick et al., 2019).

Leading in Response to Suffering

The 2018 National Policy Board for Education Administration's (NPBEA) National Educational Leadership Preparation (NELP) Standards for school- and district-level leaders brings the aim of student well-being into each academic and operational standard educators must meet in their education, development, and service as school leaders. The NELP standards simply define well-being as a student's state of being healthy, comfortable, and happy, a worthy goal for 21st-century schools despite some vocal opponents (Craig, 2009; Ecclestone & Hayes, 2008; Suissa, 2008, as cited in Popovic, 2013). The path to healthy, academically relevant schools that mold well-rounded citizens who do not just "pursue" happiness but are happy is riddled with complex dilemmas and arguments about the purposes of schooling that are at the heart of the U.S. schooling reform movement. As Hoyle and Slater (2001) noted:

> Some want schools reformed to produce high performers who become our future leaders. Others want schools that teach students how to live, share, and serve others in a world of anger, violence, poverty, and personal turmoil. Competition and high performance need not take the place of happiness, love, and service.
>
> (p. 794)

All of us who work in schools and school systems face obstacles in balancing the many reform goals of schooling. Leaders in particular face unique challenges in preparing students and working with teachers and staff in order to meet the aims of purposeful and sustainable education in the 21st century. The sought-after goal is that educational leaders maintain all the traditional elements of an academically successful school and in addition be concerned about the well-being of students, staff members, parents, and community members, AND their own well-being [NELP, 2018]. But research tells us that principals and head teachers around the world are prone to and experience high levels of stress, depression, and burnout significantly above that of other professions and the general population (DeMatthews et al. 2021; Robinson, 2018). Placing the burden of ensuring the health and well-being of a school community on a single school principal who is already facing high levels of stress means greater consideration must be paid to understanding suffering and its causes and providing education and support *to leaders* so they can serve as role models in this regard. On the one hand, healthy, disciplined lifestyles are characterized by exercise, nutrition, and a balanced social life; on the other, an intrinsic exploration linked to personal growth and values will enable school leaders to flourish themselves and also create healthy school environments (Polizzi & Ronan, 2020; Polizzi & Frick, 2012). And yet this ideal is fragile as illustrated by the most troubling aspects of a recent study of school principals in Australia that found school principals rated the level of support they derived from their employer at *less than one*, on a scale of one to ten (Robinson, 2018). The school leaders are suffering too.

Our turbulent world is crying out for strong, confident, purposeful, yet sensitive, compassionate moral leadership (Gurley & Dagley, 2020; Shapiro & Gross, 2013; Branson, 2009). Every transformational leader must do a "double take" when assessing the moral environment of the times and envision a higher purpose of schooling that becomes fundamental in transforming it (Parameshwar, 2006). Being aware of the narratives of suffering in schools and understanding how suffering manifests itself in educational practices and contexts is necessary and helpful in supporting a more complete vision of school reform and renewal.

The practice of teaching and leading involves courage inspired by many sources (Belcher, 2017; Palmer, 2007; Glickman, 2002). Leadership has countless dimensions, involving action we take physically, mentally, and spiritually, but self-protective behaviors of moral cowardice can feed suffering within organizational contexts (Leonard et al., 2014; Simola, 2016). Unless there is a moral agenda at the heart of a learning community, the school will struggle in its attempts to be an authentic learning community (Begley, 2010; Starrat, 2004). We believe if a school leader does not understand the ways in which suffering occurs in schools, they are bound to create it. Educational leaders in complex times find themselves constantly engaged in discerning the moral purpose of a community and how best to bring it alive and nurture it in a way that will allow it to shape the educational experience (Benjamin & Burford, 2021; Burford & Bezzina, 2014). Alleviating unproductive suffering in schools is an elemental component of the moral and virtuous work of educational leaders worldwide and ultimately substantiates and centers what is meant by leading for the best interests of the student (Stefkovich & Frick, 2021).

The possibility of alleviating suffering in schools is significant, and we believe it will aid in defining the integrity of an educator. As Frick and Covaleskie (2014) noted, having integrity means that a leader's professional life is guided by their core essential ethical qualities and commitments that have formed their personality. Holistic, compassionate leadership aimed at understanding and alleviating suffering encompasses a vision of school change as a movement toward inner and external harmony with the school environment rather than merely an exertion of control over it (Polizzi & Frick, 2012). A vision acknowledging this relationship between the personal self and professional practice encourages processes in the school leader that can develop inner resources toward an ethic of social cohesion. Therefore, the integrated leader in their understanding of and alleviation of the suffering of those in their community is ultimately committed to an ethic of social cohesion, both personally and professionally. An ethic of social cohesion was discussed and defined by Heuser (2005) as being built on an individual's social capital, along with the internalization of social ethics. Acting in a way to create social cohesion is a person's propensity for ethical behavior toward the common good. Heuser continued that in order for social cohesion to be sustained, each individual needs to feel autonomous to use their abilities across groups as well as organizational boundaries. We could say they have been "cohered" to a society to the extent that they act in a way that is beneficial to society overall (Heuser, 2005, p. 8). Inner resources aimed toward social cohesion allow for sustainable self-reliance and increased professional competence by a deepening understanding of one's own motivations. Through this, a practice unfurls based in dialogue and discourse about the relevance of reflection, understanding, and alleviating suffering in order to pursue the compassionate response. The compassionate educator who seeks to understand and alleviate another's suffering simultaneously displays a strong sense of personal and professional integrity while remaining focused outward on the search of creating a caring environment, across organizational boundaries, for the suffering person. Ultimately, the community as a whole enables *flourishing* as a basic reality of the dynamic functionality of the school.

Identifying, being aware, and seeking to understand suffering in schools while working to alleviate it is a virtuous ethical commitment informed and grounded in the aims of social cohesion. In the democratic realm, educators' intimate encounters with students' sufferings make them more responsible citizens and awaken their awareness of the pressing, quiet needs of others. In conclusion, we want to clear an open space for an ability to reflect on the role; learning humility, grace, fortitude, and compassion are part of the realm of educational leadership. Doing so will help enable growth in the areas of moral purpose and courage, and ultimately instill a sense of hope in schools.

References

Adelman, H., & Taylor, L. (2021). *Embedding mental health as schools change.* Center for Mental Health in Schools & Student/Learning Supports. University of California Los Angeles.

Aeschylus. (1961). *Agamemmnon. The Agamemnon of Aeschylus* (G. Murray, trans.). G. Allen & Unwin Ltd. (Original work published 458 BCE).

American Humanist Association. (2021). *Definition of humanism.* https://americanhumanist.org/what-is-humanism/definition-of-humanism/

Anderson, G., & Cohen, M. I. (2015). Redesigning the identities of teachers an leaders: A framework for studying new professionalism and educator resistance. *Education Policy Analysis Archives, 23*(85), 1–29.

Baker, D. (2014). *The schooled society: The education transformation of global culture.* Stanford University Press.

Balzer, W. E., & Frick, W. C. (2017, October). *An analysis of safety and responsiveness policies and school leadership in the prevention of child sexual abuse by school volunteers.* Paper presented at the Rocky Mountain Educational Research Association, Lawton, Oklahoma.

Begley, P.T. (2010). Leading with moral purpose: The place of ethics. In T. Bush, L. Bell, & D. Middlewood (Eds.). *The principles of educational leadership & management.* (pp. 31–54). SAGE Publications.

Belcher, D. (2017). Moral leadership in an age of school accountability. *Journal of Leadership Studies, 11,* 60–62. https://doi.org/10.1002/jls.21528

Benjamin, A., & Burford, C. (2021). *Leadership in a synodal church.* Garratt Publishing.

Bichell, R. E. (2016). *Suicide rates climb in the US, especially among adolescent girls.* NPR Radio.   http://www.npr.org/sections/health-shots/2016/04/22/474888854/suicide-rates-climb-in-u-s-especially-among-adolescent-girls

Branson, C. (2009). *Leadership for an age of wisdom.* Springer Educational Publishing.

Brasof, M. (2015). *Student voice and school governance: Distributing leadership to youth and adults.* Routledge

Burford, C. & Bezzina, M. (2014). Striving for moral purpose. In C. Branson & S. J. Gross (Eds.), *Handbook of ethical educational leadership* (pp. 405–425). Routledge.

CASEL (2019). *Fundamentals of SEL.* https://casel.org/fundamentals-of-sel/

Charmaz, K. (1999). Stories of suffering; subjective tales and research narratives. *Qualitative Health Researcher, 9*(3), 362–382.

Corradi-Fiumara, G. (2015). *Psychic suffering: from pain to growth.* London: Karnac Books.

Craig, C. (2009). *Well-being in schools: the curious case of the tail wagging the dog?* Center for Confidence and Well-being.

Crain, T. (2016, September). *Why did Alabama paddle 19,000 students in one year?* Alabama School Connection. http://alabamaschoolconnection.org/page/4/

Davies, J. (2012). *The Importance of suffering: The value and meaning of emotional discontent.* Routledge.

DeMatthews, D., Carrola, P., Reyes, P., & Knight, D. (2021). School leadership burnout and job-related stress: Recommendations for district administrators and principals. *The Clearing House: A Journal of Educational Strategies, Issues and Ideas, 94*(4), 15967. https://doi.org/10.1080/00098655.2021.1894083

Denizet-Lewis, B. (2017) Why are more American teenagers suffering from severe anxiety? *The New York Times.* https://www.nytimes.com/2017/10/11/magazine/why-are-more-american-teenagers-than-ever-suffering-from-severe-anxiety.html

Diliberti, M.K. & Schwartz, H.L. (2022). District Leaders' Concerns About Mental Health and Political Polarization in Schools: Selected Findings from the Fourth American School District Panel Survey. RR-A956-8. Rand Corporation. DOI: https://doi.org/10.7249/RRA956-8

Dodge, R., Daly, A., Huyton, J., & Sanders, L. (2012). The challenge of defining well-being. *International Journal of Well-being, 2*(3), 222–235.

Eades, J., Proctor C., & Ashley, M. (2014). Happiness in the classroom. In S. David, I. Boniwell, & A. Conley Ayers (Eds.), *The Oxford handbook of happiness* (pp. 579–591). Oxford University Press

Ecclestone, K., & Hayes, D. (2008) Affect: knowledge, communication, creativity and emotion, Beyond Current Horizons. http://www.beyondcurrenthorizons.org.uk/affectknowledge-communication-creativity-and-emotion/

Fitzpatrick, S., Kerridge, I., Jordens, C., Zoloth, L., Tollefsen, C., Tsomo, K. L., Jensen, M., Sachedina, A., & Sarma, D. (2016). Religious perspectives on human suffering: implications for medicine and bioethics. *Journal of Religion and Health, 55*(1),159–173.

Florida State Board of Education. (2019). *Action item.* https://www.fldoe.org/core/fileparse.php/18786/urlt/6A1-094121.pdf

Frank, A. W. (2001). Can we research suffering? *Qualitative Health Research, 11*(3), 353–362. https://doi.org/10.1177/104973201129119154

Fredricks, J. A., Parr, A. K., Amemiya, J. L., Wang, M.-T., & Brauer, S. (2019). What matters for urban adolescents' engagement and disengagement in school: A mixed-methods study. *Journal of Adolescent Research, 34*(5), 491–527. https://doi.org/10.1177/0743558419830638

Frick, W. C. (2011). Practicing a professional ethic: Leading for students' best interests. *American Journal of Education, 117*, 527–562. https://doi.org/10.1086/660757

Frick, W. C. & Covaleskie, J. F. (2014). Preparation for integrity. In C. Branson & S. J. Gross (Eds.), *Handbook of ethical educational leadership* (pp. 386-404). Routledge.

Frick, W., Parson, J., & Frick, E. (2019). Disarming privilege to achieve equitable school communities: A spiritually-attuned school leadership response to our storied lives. *Interchange, 50*, 549–568.

Gibbons, S., & Silva, O. (2008). *School quality, child well-being and parents' satisfaction.* Centre for Economics of Education.

Ginwright, S. (2018, May 31). *The future of healing: shifting from trauma informed care to healing centered engagement.* Medium. https://medium.com/@ginwright/the-future-of-healing-shifting-from-trauma-informed-care-to-healing-centered-engagement-634f557ce69c

Glickman, C. (2002). The courage to lead. *Educational Leadership, 59*(8), 41–44.

Gurley, D. K., & Dagley, A. (2020). Pulling back the curtain on moral reasoning and ethical leadership development for K–12 school leaders. *Journal of Research on Leadership Education, 16*(3), 243–274. https://doi.org/10.1177/1942775120921213

Habito, R. (2004). *Living Zen, loving God.* Wisdom Publications.

Hase, C. N., Goldberg, S. B., Smith, D., Stuck, A., & Campain, J. (2015). Impacts of traditional bullying and cyberbullying on the mental health of middle school and high school students. *Psychology in the Schools, 52*(6), 607–617.

Heuser, B.L. (2005). The ethics of social cohesion. *Peabody Journal of Education, 80*(4), 8–15. https://doi.org/10.1207/S15327930pje8004_2

Hoyle, J.R. & Slater, R.O. (2001). Love, happiness, and America's schools: The role of educational leadership in the 21st century. *The Phi Delta Kappan, 82*(10), 790–794

Kundu, P. (2018, July 17). *"Happiness Curriculum" introduced in Delhi govt schools: In world obsessed with marks, studies can still be source of joy.* First Post. https://www.firstpost.com/india/happiness-curriculum-introduced-in-delhi-govt-schools-in-a-world-obsessed-with-marks-studies-can-still-be-a-source-of-joy-4755651.html

Leonard, P. E., Schilling, T., & Normore, A. H. (2014). Holistic moral development of educational leaders. In C. Branson & S. J. Gross (Eds.), *Handbook of ethical educational leadership* (pp. 315–336). Routledge.

Maiti, A. (2021). Effect of corporal punishment on young children's educational outcomes. *Education Economics*, 1–13

Mintz, A. (2012). The Happy and suffering student? Rousseau's Emile and the path not taken in progressive educational thought. *Educational Theory, 62*(3), 249–265.

Nesi, J., & Prinstein, M. J. (2015). Using social media for social comparison and feedback-seeking: Gender and popularity moderate associations with depressive symptoms. *Journal of Abnormal Child Psychology, 43*(8), 1427–1438.

New York State Education Department. (2018). *Mental health education literacy in schools: linking to a continuum of well-being.* http://www.nysed.gov/common/nysed/files/programs/curriculum-instruction/continuumofwellbeingguide.pdf

NPBEA. (2018). *National Educational Leadership Preparation (NELP) Program Standards–Building Level.* http://www.npbea.org/

Palmer, P. (2007). *The courage to teach: Exploring the inner landscape of a teacher's life.* Wiley.

Parameshwar, S. (2006). Inventing higher purpose through suffering: The transformation of the transformational leader. *The Leadership Quarterly, 17,* 454–474.

Pinckaers, S. (2015). *Passions and virtues.* The Catholic University of America Press.

Polizzi, J., & Frick, W. (2012). Transformative preparation and professional development: authentic reflective practice for school leaders. *Teaching & Learning,* 26(1), 20–34.

Polizzi, J., & Ronan, D. (2020). Contemplation for educators: theoretical, ethical and practical dimensions drawn from the Catholic intellectual tradition. *Values and Ethics in Educational Administration, 15*(2). http://www.ucea.org/initiatives/ucea-centre-study-leadership-ethics/

Popovic, N. (2013). Should education have happiness lessons? In S. David, I. Boniwell, & A. Conley Ayers (Eds.), *The Oxford handbook of happiness* (pp. 551–562) Oxford University Press.

Robinson, N. (2018). *School principals at higher risk of burnout, depression due to workplace stress, survey finds.* https://www.abc.net.au/news/2018-02-21/principals-overwhelmed-by-workplace-stress-acu-survey-finds/9468078

Sahlberg, P. (2012). *How GERM is infecting schools around the world?* [Blog post]. https://pasisahlberg.com/text-test/

Saturn, S. (2017). Two factors that fuel compassion: The oxytocin system and the social experience of moral elevation. In E. Seppälä, E. Simon-Thomas, S. Brown, M. Worline, D. Cameron, & J. Doty (Eds.), *The Oxford handbook of compassion science* (pp 121-131). Oxford University Press.

Schohaus, W. (2012/1932). *The dark places of education* (M. Chadwick, Trans.) Routledge. (Original work published 1930).

Shapiro, J. P., & Gross, S. J. (2013). *Ethical educational leadership in turbulent times: (re)solving moral dilemmas.* Routledge.

Shapiro, J. P., & Stefkovich, J. A. (2016). *Ethical leadership and decision making in education.* Routledge.

Simola, S. (2016), Mentoring the morally courageous: a relational cultural perspective, *Career Development International, 21*(4), 340–354. https://doi.org/10.1108/CDI-01-2016-0010

Starrat, J. (2004). *Ethical leadership.* Jossey Bass.

Stefkovich, J. & Frick, W. (2021). *The best interest of the student: Applying ethical constructs to legal cases in education.* Routledge.

Stratham, J., & Chase, E. (2010). *Childhood Well-being: A brief overview* [Briefing Paper]. Childhood Well-being Research Center.

Taylor, R., & Watson, J. (1989). *They shall not hurt: Human suffering and human caring.* Colorado Associated University Press.

Todd, S. (2002). Listening as attending to the "echo of the otherwise": On suffering, justice, and education. *Philosophy of Education Yearbook,* 405-412.

Vachon, D. D., Kruegar, R. F., Rogosch, F. A., & Cicchetti, D. (2015). Assessment of harmful psychiatric and behavioral effects of different forms of child maltreatment. *JAMA Psychiatry, 72*(11), 1–9.

Vestal, C. (2018, June 23). *States begin requiring mental health education in schools.* https://namivirginia.org/states-begin-requiring-mental-health-education-schools/

Wilkinson, I. (2005). *Suffering: A sociological introduction.* Polity Press.

Wilkinson, I., & Kleinman, A. (2016). *A passion for society: how we think about human suffering*. University of California Press.

World Health Organization. (2017, March 30). *"Depression: Let's talk" says WHO, as depression tops list of causes of ill health*. [Press release]. https://www.who.int/news-room/detail/30-03-2017--depression-let-s-talk-says-who-as-depression-tops-list-of-causes-of-ill-health

Younger, J. B. (1995). The alienation of the sufferer. *Advances in Nursing Science, 17*(4), 53–72.

2 Willi Schohaus and the *Shadow over the School*

Suffering Then...

If the teachers had a sense of class, they would buy the book and burn it publicly.[1]

Introduction

Dr. Willi Schohaus, a 31-year-old professor of psychology and pedagogy at the Lehrerseminar (Teacher's Seminary or Teachers' Institute) in Rorschach, Switzerland, posed the question, "From what did you suffer most in school?"[2] The call for responses appeared in the October and November 1927 editions of *Schweizer-Spiegel*, a popular German language, Swiss monthly magazine of culture and politics, comparable to *Reader's Digest* in the United States (Figure 2.1 and 2.2).

Schohaus's article directed readers to send their answers to the editor by the end of the month. *Schweizer-Spiegel* received hundreds of replies from a cross-section of Swiss people. The magazine published selected accounts and corresponding commentary in the December 1927 Christmas issue, with additional narratives published in the January and February 1928 issues (Figure 2.3).

Taking all four issues together, a challenging discussion ensued on the purpose of schooling, the nature of teaching, and the hardships faced by students. The educational soul-searching that Schohaus sparked was not without strong opinions. For example, more than 400 people canceled their subscriptions to the magazine because they were so offended by the question.[3] Meanwhile, on February 28, 1928, Schohaus secured the directorship of teacher training in Kreuzlingen, a school that maintains a long history in Swiss teacher education to this day. Schohaus already gained a reputation as a Pestalozzi scholar by publishing three volumes of his letters, but it was the publication of his *Schatten über der Schule* (*Shadow over the School*, an extension of his *Schweizer-Spiegel* articles) in 1930 that firmly established Schohaus as an educational progressive and practical humanist of international reputation. A translation of *Schatten über der Schule* appeared in English in 1932, as *The Dark Places of Education*.

This chapter contextualizes the life and times of Dr. Willi Schohaus. It discusses progressive education and school reform in Switzerland in the first half of the 20th century, provides a brief biographical sketch of Schohaus and outlines his pedagogical ideals, discusses the impact of his seminal work, *Schatten über der Schule*, and introduces 13 themes of suffering in schools that characterized his original study.

DOI: 10.4324/9780429465499-2

Figure 2.1 Original call for responses from the October 1927 edition of *Schweizer Spiegel*

Context of Education in Switzerland Early 1900s

Throughout the early part of the 20th century, progressive education movements were inspired by the Enlightenment and part of broader reform movements in Western society that sought to alleviate suffering and promote moral and intellectual advancement (Reese, 2001). In 1899, Adolphe Ferriére, son of a noted Swiss doctor and a vice president of the International Red Cross, founded the International Bureau of New Schools in Switzerland at Les Pleiades-sur-Blonay in the Canton of Vaud (Stewart, 1968; Brehony, 2006). The Bureau of New Schools played a central role in establishing the progressive education movement in Switzerland.

In 1921 Ferriére, along with Beatrice Breony and Elisabeth Rotten, established the New Education Fellowship (NEF) (Brehony, 2006). The NEF and The New Era in Home and Schools were influential associations during this time and served as the global home to the earlier ideals of Rousseau, Pestalozzi, 19th-century humanists, and the new ideas of Piaget, Dewey, Montessori, and other

Dr.
W. Schohaus
Lehrer für Pädagogik
am Seminar Rorschach

Unsere
neue Rundfrage

WORUNTER HABEN SIE IN DER SCHULE AM MEISTEN GELITTEN?

Wir wiederholen unsere Umfrage in dieser Nummer noch einmal, um den Lesern und Leserinnen Gelegenheit zur Beteiligung zu bieten, die eigentlich antworten wollten, denen es aber bisher an Zeit, an geeigneter Stimmung oder ausreichender Willensspannung fehlte.

Das Problem m u s s jedermann interessieren ! — Die Schule entscheidet so weitgehend über Wohl und Wehe der Jugendzeit. Und von den Eindrücken der Jugend hängt in so hohem Masse Tüchtigkeit, Glück und Sinn unseres Lebens ab.

Die relativ grosse Uninteressiertheit der Erwachsenen ist das grösste Hemmnis für eine erfreuliche Entwicklung der Schule.

Schreiben Sie uns, worin die Schule I h n e n gegenüber erzieherisch versagt hat !

Schreiben Sie uns von den Schulnöten I h r e r Kinder !

Und denken Sie daran : Die Unzulänglichkeiten liegen nicht nur an dem, was die Schule « falsch macht », sondern weitgehend auch an dem, w a s s i e

Figure 2.2 Second call for responses from the November 2, 1927, edition of *Schweizer Spiegel*

unterlässt, in der Vernachlässigung oder im völligen Ignorieren von Auf-
gaben, denen sie vernünftigerweise gerecht werden sollte.

Es handelt sich auch nicht nur um Tatbestände, unter denen die Kinder
b e w u s s t leiden. Der Schuldruck schafft vielfach Verhältnisse, die von den
Kindern in dumpfem Fatalismus als unabänderlich hingenommen werden, weil
sie gar nicht ahnen, w i e tatenfroh, frei und heiter die Jugendzeit eigentlich
sein könnte. Solche Einsicht kommt meist erst in spätern Jahren.

Schildern Sie die Nöte möglichst konkret und anschaulich an B e i s p i e -
l e n. Aber vergessen Sie darüber nicht, dass die a l l g e m e i n e B e g r ü n -
d u n g jener Leiden noch wichtiger ist. Versuchen Sie, Ihre Kritik zusammen-
zufassen und zu verallgemeinern. Stellen Sie sich die Frage auch so : W e l c h e s
s i n d d i e b e d e n k l i c h s t e n u n d v e r b r e i t e t s t e n S c h a t t e n -
s e i t e n u n s e r e s S c h u l w e s e n s ? —

Schreiben Sie ausführlich ! Für den Fall der Veröffentlichung wird es uns
nicht schwer sein, zweckmässig zu kürzen.

I m ü b r i g e n n o c h m a l s :

Keine Personennamen nennen, wohl aber Ort und Typus der Schule an-
geben, von der Sie Einzelheiten berichten. Auch ungefähre Zeitangaben sind
wichtig.

Die Veröffentlichungen werden anonym erscheinen; ebenso werden alle
Indiskretionen streng vermieden. Veröffentlichte Beiträge werden honoriert.

Die A n t w o r t e n sind an die Redaktion des « Schweizer-Spiegel », Zürich 1, Storchengasse 16, zu senden.

Die E i n s e n d e f r i s t ist bis zum 15. November 1927 verlängert worden.

Figure 2.2 (Continued)

WORUNTER
haben Sie in der Schule am meisten gelitten?

Das Ergebnis der Rundfrage

von Dr. W. Schohaus, Lehrer für Psychologie
und Pädagogik am Seminar Rorschach

Die Antworten auf unsere Rundfrage haben ein erschütterndes Material zutage gefördert. Selbst die kleine Auswahl, die wir im « Schweizer-Spiegel » publizieren können, legt davon Zeugnis ab. Es ist selbstverständlich, dass sich die Veröffentlichung dieser furchtbaren Anklagen nicht gegen die Lehrerschaft als Gesamtheit wendet. Eine solche Missdeutung verbieten schon Stellung und Ruf des Verfassers, Dr. W. Schohaus. Ausserdem wird dem « Schweizer-Spiegel » niemand zutrauen, dass er, dessen höchstes Ziel es ist, mitzuhelfen, dass wir uns untereinander besser verstehen, einen Stand herausgreifen würde, um diesen als solchen anzugreifen.

Wir wissen, welch schweren und verantwortungsvollen Beruf der Lehrer mit seinem Amt übernimmt. Wir wissen, dass es überall Lehrer gibt, die ihrem Beruf mit grosser Selbsthingabe dienen. Ueberdies leidet ja nicht nur das Kind unter den Mängeln der Schule, sondern auch der gute Lehrer. Wie oft ist gerade er ein Opfer des Schulhasses, den schlechte Lehrer oder falsche Schulsysteme verschuldet haben! Wir halten es für bedeutsam, dass verhältnismässig so viele Lehrer und Lehrerinnen selbst Leidensbeiträge zu unserer Rundfrage geleistet haben. Es ist auch kein Zufall, dass die nachfolgenden Zeilen gerade von einem Lehrer geschrieben sind:

« Gewiss muss das Schulproblem jedermann interessieren, am meisten wohl den, der seinerzeit gelitten hat, heute aber selbst vor einer Klasse steht und dem nur der eine Wunsch auf der Seele brennt, seinen Kindern viel zu sein, seine ihm anvertraute Kinderschar intellektuell zu fördern, ihre Seelennöte zu erforschen und zu beheben, sie zu sittlich-starken Menschen zu gestalten… Und wenn es dem « Schweizer-Spiegel » durch seine Frage auch nur gelingen sollte, da und dort einen Lehrer oder Eltern zu veranlassen, in sich zu gehen und sich ihrer hohen Aufgabe bewusst zu werden, dann hat er schon Grosses vollbracht, und wenn dadurch auch nur ein Kind weniger zu leiden hätte. »

Alle Schulnot lässt sich auf drei Grundursachen zurückführen: Sie liegt erstens im System unserer Schule, in der Macht einer vielfach verknöcherten Tradition, der gegenüber auch der Lehrer als einzelner ohnmächtig ist.

Sie liegt zum andern Teil und hauptsächlich in der Tatsache, dass im Lehrerberuf häufig Leute wirken, denen

Figure 2.3 Reader accounts from the December 1927 edition of *Schweizer Spiegel*

eine genügende pädagogische Qualifi-
kation abgesprochen werden muss.

Oft liegt die Quelle des Leidens aber
auch in erster Linie beim Kinde
selbst, in seiner Ueberempfindlichkeit,
in seinem verträumten Wesen, in seiner
mangelhaften Selbstdisziplin, in seiner
übersteigerten Liebebedürftigkeit, in seinem zähen Festhalten an unerfüllbaren
romantischen Erwartungen.

In diesen letzten Fällen wird es durch-
wegs an der häuslichen Erziehung des vorschulpflichtigen Alters ge-
fehlt haben. Wir müssen uns immer die
Tatsache gegenwärtig halten, dass sich
eben notwendig die meisten elterlichen
Erziehungsfehler im Schulleben rächen
müssen; sonst werden wir gegen Lehrer
und Schule ungerecht.

Im besondern kristallieren sich aus den
Einsendungen die nachfolgenden Mo-
mente heraus, die dem Schulleiden am
häufigsten zugrunde liegen:

1. Mangelnde Heiterkeit und
   Geltungshunger des Lehrers
   (humorlose Disziplin, einengender
   Zwang, Misstrauen, Gereiztheit, Pe-
   danterie).

2. Sarkasmus, Spott und Hohn
   des Lehrers, Angst der Kinder vor
   dem Ausgelachtwerden und Verstär-
   kung von Minderwertigkeitsaffekten.

3. Ungerechtigkeit und besonders
   Parteilichkeit des Lehrers, Er-
   schütterung des kindlichen Vertrauens,
   Verwöhnungen und kränkende Ver-
   nachlässigungen.

4. Verständnislosigkeit und
   Uninteressiertheit des Leh-
   rers gegenüber einzelnen oder allen
   Schülern.

5. Körperstrafen, Gefühl der Er-
   niedrigung und des Ausgeliefertseins
   bei den Schülern.

6. Allgemeine Stoffüberbürdung
   und Leiden der Schüler an der Unzu-
   länglichkeit einem oder mehreren be-
   stimmten Fächern gegenüber.

7. Angst und Gefährdung des Selbstver-
   trauens durch Hausaufgaben,
   Klausuren, Prüfungen, Zen-
   suren und Zeugnisse.

8. Mangelnde Entfaltung der Ka-
   meradschaft in der Klasse.

Die nachfolgenden Beispiele sind im
Sinne dieser Uebersicht ausgewählt und
geordnet worden. Jeder Brief soll möglichst einen dieser Tatbestände gut ver-
anschaulichen. — Die Wahl gab uns viel
zu schaffen, da die Fülle der Einsendungen ausserordentlich gross ist, und weil
wir hier nichts darstellen wollen, was
nicht durch viele der eingegangenen
Dokumente belegt werden könnte.

Wir beginnen mit einem Bekenntnis,
in dem die charakteristische Reaktion
freiheitsdurstiger und liebehungriger Jugend gegen kühle Nüchternheit und hu-
morlosen Zwang Ausdruck findet. Der
Bericht stammt, nebenbei gesagt, aus der
Feder eines sehr bekannten schweizeri-
schen Schriftstellers:

Die Antwort lautet bei mir klipp und
klar: Unter der «Autorität» der Lehrer.
Es ist und war ganz zweifellos die Gewalt
dieser Herrschenden, und zwar habe ich
bis in mein letztes Schuljahr vierte Klasse
Realschule gezittert und geängstet unter
der Macht dieser furchtbaren Herren! —
In diesem allerletzten Schuljahr aber, da
wir das vierzehnte Altersjahr überschritten
hatten, war plötzlich der Bann gebrochen,
behandelten uns die Lehrer als Menschen,

Figure 2.3 (Continued)

educators of the epoch. They sought educational reforms based on a scientific understanding of the child and a desire to reverse long-standing educational logic (Haenggeli-Jenni, 2016). As surmised by Hofstetter and Schneuwly (2006), the new school era was an internal one, based in the new field of psychology and its methodology that incorporated observation, description, experimental processes, measurement, and the determining of children's aptitudes. The new paradigm that began to take hold was a holistic understanding of the child in myriad ways.

Understanding the whole child in the context of the primary and/or secondary school as an institution was at the front of the progressive educational undertaking. New Era educators emphasized that primary and secondary schooling had other aims besides the purely academic. How a child learns—the child's psychological, social, physical, emotionally natural development —became a matter of principal importance and study. The teacher's role was presented as one who understands the nature and psychology of children, including their humanistic elements such as sentiments, instincts, and feelings. These ideals were at the center of the moment. The pedagogical methods in turn presented students with the contexts for character development and learning on their own, with a nurturing teacher at the helm in a socially supportive environment. Other reversals of the prevailing logic of the time, according to Reese, which are now common educational practice,

> were that children were considered to be active not passive learners; they are innocent and good and not fallen ... that early education was relevant, and instrumental to outcomes in life; the natural world and not necessarily books were the best teacher; kindness, benevolence and hard work—not stern discipline, harsh rebukes or corporal punishment were the best forms of discipline and that the traditional curriculum was medieval, mind numbing, unnatural and pernicious—essentially a sin against childhood.
>
> (2001, p. 2)

The NEF's origination dates back to 1914 when The Conference for New Ideals in Education took place in Letchworth, England (Stewart, 1968). Three journals affiliated with the organization that were international in scope included *The New Era, Pour L'Ere Nouvelle,* and *Das Werdende Zeitaler,* covering three of the major European languages. In 1922 the three journals published substantially similar statements on the principles of the NEF that appeared in each issue of the respective journals until 1932. The principles were:

1. The essential aim of all education is to prepare the child to seek and realize in his own life the supremacy of the spirit. Whatever other view the educator may take, education should aim at maintaining and increasing spiritual energy in the child.
2. Education should respect the child's individuality. This individuality can only be developed by means of a discipline which sets free the spiritual powers within him.

3. The studies, and indeed the whole training for life, should give free play to the child's innate interests—interests which awaken spontaneously in him and find their expression in various intellectual, aesthetic, social and other activities.

4. Each age has its own special character. For this reason, individual corporate disciplines need to be organized by the children themselves in collaboration with their teachers. These disciplines should make for a deeper sense of individual and social responsibility.

5. Selfish competition must disappear from education and be replaced by co-operation which teaches the child to put himself at the service of his community.

6. Co-education—instruction and education in common—does not mean the identical treatment of the two sexes, but a collaboration which allows each sex to exercise a salutary influence on the other.

7. The New Education fits the child to become not only a citizen capable of doing his duties to his neighbours, his nation and humanity at large, but a human being conscious of his personal dignity. (Stewart, 1968)

These progressive ideals proliferated from the NEF, centered in Europe, and had global reach. NEF conferences had affiliated organizations around the world, including such places as Australia, Bahamas, Belgium, China, Denmark, Finland, France, Iraq, Iceland, Japan, Switzerland, and more. Schools around the world such as Dewey's *Lab* in Chicago, Montessori's *Casa dei Bambini* in Rome, Geheeb's *Oldenwalschule* in Germany and then Switzerland, A. S. Neill's *Summerhill* in England, Hahn's *Salem Schools* in Germany and Great Britain, and other progressive, democratically oriented, child-centered schools took into account the reality of the social child.and encouraged their own initiative aimed at a harmonious development of the soul, the mind, and the body of the child (Grunder, 2011). This call began to define an authentic, child-centered moment in education, driven by a deep humane understanding of children's lives and the serious role that school's play in their full development.

Willi Schohaus

Schohaus was born in Zurich, Switzerland, on February 1, 1897, to German parents. His father, Eugene, was a merchant originally from Westphalia and his mother, Clara, was from Cologne. His early school experiences were not happy ones. Bored in elementary school and expelled from the Zurich Cantonal School in 1915, he was able to graduate through The Minerva Institute, a Swiss vocational school, and pass his Matura exam, the Swiss equivalent to the *Abitur* (secondary education qualification). He went on to study theology for one semester in Berlin and soon after served in the German army during World War I, seeing combat in France and Belgium in 1917 and 1918. Returning to Switzerland in 1919 at the age of 22, Schohaus settled in Bern, a city located in the same region where Pestalozzi had his apprenticeship in modern farming and his first school for children a century before (Trohler, 2001). At the University of Bern,

Schohaus studied philosophy, psychology, and pedagogy under Paul Häberlin,[4] who had a background in zoology and botany as well as philosophy, and who previously served as the Kreuzlingen Thurgau Seminary director (1904–1909). Häberlin oversaw Schohaus's doctoral thesis, titled *Die theoretischen Grundlagen und die wissenschaftstheoretische Stellung der Psychonalysis* [*The Theoretical Foundations and Scientific Theory of Psychoanalysis*] (1923). Graduating from the University of Bern in 1922, in 1924/25, Schohaus, like Pestalozzi, led a private school in Muri, near Bern, for children difficult to educate. This was followed by a teaching post at the Lehrerseminar in Rorschach, where he published Pestalozzi's letters in an accessible form titled *Pestalozzi Werke: Secular Edition in 3 Volumes* (Kobi, 1981; Schohaus, 1927a, 1927b). The Government Council of the Canton of Thurgau elected him to the position of Director of the Lehrerseminar in Kreuzlingen on February 28, 1928. His duties included a teaching assignment in education, psychology, and Protestant religion. In his curriculum vitae submitted for the position, Schohaus noted, "I am interested in development and child psychology and have great interest in the practical application of these disciplines in the field of education" (Frick, 1962). Around the time of publication of *Schatten über der Schule* in 1932, he married Heidi Weiss. She was his support and confidant throughout his career, and the couple aided refugee educators settling in Switzerland during the interwar period. In 1932, George Unwin Press published an English translation of *Schatten über der Schule* as *The Dark Places of Education*.

In 1932 Schohaus also partnered with architects from Congres Internationaux d'Architecture Moderne (CIAM) and the health reform activist from the University of Zurich, Wilhelm von Gonzenbach, to present the didactic exhibition *Der neu Schulbau* [*The New School Building*] in Zurich, Switzerland, which showcased the marriage of progressive pedagogy, medical expertise, and modernist architecture (Kinchin, 1999). Together with his collaborators on the exhibition, he published *Das Kind und sein schulhaus: Ein Beitrag zur Reform Schulhausbaues* [*The Child and the School Building*] in 1933. Using a similar methodology as he did with *Dark Places*, he also published in 1933 *Der Lehrer von heute und sein schwerer Beruf: mit 27im text zitierten Beckenntnissen von Lehren und ihre Berufsnöte* [*The Teacher of Today and His Difficult Profession: With 27 Quoted In-text Confessions of Teachers and Their Professional Needs*]. He published *Seele und Beruf des Lehres* [*The Soul and Profession of the Teacher*] in 1938 (Figure 2.4).

Schohaus retired in 1962, having served 34 years as the Lehrerseminar Kreuzlingen director. Upon his retirement, the school dedicated a special issue of the school yearbook to him. According to Jacob Müller (1962), a government councilor,

> Dr. Schohaus was a personality who knew what he wanted, not only did he know Pestalozzi's works thoroughly, but he also worked in his mind and his spirit; he endeavored to educate the prospective teachers into men and women who regarded themselves as servants of the youth and who could find their way in the environment in which they might be placed.

(p. 8)

Figure 2.4 Photograph of Willi Schohaus around the time that *The Dark Places of Education* was published

Schohaus continued to write in his retirement, issuing his final text, *Erziehung zur Menschlikeit: ein Buch fur Eltern und Lehrer [Education for Humanity: A Book for Parents and Teachers]* in 1969. He died in Zurich on June 22, 1981, at the age of 85. According to his obituary, "What Schohaus was able to do in his writing, however, with all the sharp and undisguised critique, what distinguished him from the reformist bustle of the time, was his rational control, aesthetic for moderation and his forgiving mirth" (Kobi, 1981, p. 36). Schohaus, maintaining his position as Lehrerseminar director for over three decades, prepared many, many hundreds of teachers in a humanistic pedagogy we still seek today.

Pedagogical Ideals and Practices

In reading through Schohaus's work, and examining his life, it became clear to us that the ideals and practices advanced by him were, and still are to this day, fundamental to what effective schooling must be. With the growth, development, and blossoming of the field of psychology in Europe and around the world in the early part of the 20th century, Schohaus sought to incorporate and apply natural, humanistic psychology to the solving of educational problems (and we can see the very same contemporary efforts as explained in Chapter 1).

As director, he instituted a less regimented, yet still disciplined, classroom environment where self-governance pervaded and a more casual, informal, and social relationship between the teacher and students was enacted. This approach was a component part of teacher training in Kreuzlingen, where the first director, Jakob Wehrli, served from 1833 to 1853 and instituted Pestalozzi's method of holistic education as founding precepts (Isler, 2008). Learning took place in a community Schohaus organized around hard work, camaraderie, sincerity, and carefully practiced and studied leisure that included an appreciation for nature and the arts. The term *lebengemeinshaft*, meaning partnership, or living community, and sometimes used in reference to civil unions, is relevant here to explain the importance of the teacher–student relationship implied and enacted in the context of Schohaus's *lehrerseminar*. Excursions outside of the classroom and into the local community encouraged teacher and students to learn experientially, physically, and socially. Schohaus played down didactic and rote approaches. Hands-on-apprenticeships, social utility, and student engagement with real-life scenarios were instrumental to the aims of progressive, *gemeinschaft*-oriented, liberal educators, in which group Schohaus was included. He also considered the school as a physical structure subject to necessary design considerations, rather than mirroring a panopticon-like factory, popular at this time. He promoted architecture that opened schools up to the outdoors and natural light. He wished for schools to be community-oriented, aesthetically pleasing, healthy, and wholesome places.

Schohaus's progressive, humanistic idealism challenged the regimented and constrained nature of schools, and this challenge continued throughout the 34 years he served as *lehrerseminar* director in Kreuzlingen. He argued that many types of learners, artists as well as common people, found the coercion and mental uniformity of the school a tormenting environment: "The school puts shackles on the emerging genius" (Schohaus, 1927a, 1927b, p. 58). He criticized teacher grade books and contrasted them to "the power of a good poem; able to touch the deepest wounds and affecting a child's self-confidence by keeping them in fearful tension of the teacher's instructions, classroom and the school" (Schohaus, 1932, p. 48). To Schohaus, the traditional teacher's focus on the middling range of student ability slowed the progress of advanced students and left others to fall behind. Pestalozzi's method, embraced by Schohaus, sought freedom in autonomy for one and all (Soëtard, 1994), and Schohaus, in this same light, believed "the chief thing is that the child should observe correctly and learn to make his own deductions whenever possible" (Schohaus, 1932, p. 48).

Schohaus was particularly keen to remove corporal punishment from the schools. He exposed the ferocity of the beatings, thrashings, and "boxing of the ears" that children received at the hand of vicious teachers as a disciplinary measure. He scorned and clarified the inherent inhumanity of corporal punishment and its negative effects on students and on the principles of education. At its core, coupled with the practical, popular, and realistic appeal for responses from all persons, Schohaus's question, "From what did you suffer most in school?" was and remains a moral one: the aim of his analysis of the respondents' answers was to impact the culture of how learning occurs and make schools more compassionate, humane, democratic, and joyful institutions. He was not seeking to instill virtuous high-minded platitudes, but rather aimed his understanding at the commonality of schooling as experienced by students themselves with a goal of finding answers to timeless, practical questions and concerns of teaching and learning.

Aesthetic Education

As Pestalozzi's practical disciple in the New Era's scientific climate, Schohaus's pedagogical aim was to educate the head, heart, and hand in a rational manner, incorporating his own philosophy of spiritual and aesthetic education that defined his humane work. As Lehrerseminar director, his practice adhered to the central aspect that remains the spirit of the Pestalozzi method evident in the challenges he brought forth. While his philosophy was democratic, humanistic, and ethical, he nevertheless taught and wrote with a critical attitude and palpable irony. His writing and teaching were inherently idealist and challenging to technocratic conservatives (Kobi, 1981). One of Schohaus's guideposts was a belief in aesthetic education that informed the moral tendencies and classroom practices of his work and gave perspective to his students. His belief was that moralism was doomed to failure: both the way in which a conservative's pursuit of the preservation of existing conditions and the liberal's demand for a better world can cause more evil than blessings.[5] Schohaus's resolution to this inherent dilemma was not only practical, by asking timeless questions, but also included an aesthetic vision of the purpose of education. Schohaus certainly valued religion and spirituality—and his views spanned religions, rather than being linked to particular dogmas, as a foundational aspect of an aesthetic and humanistic education.

Schohaus maintained a reverence for artistic expression and included it as a component of teacher education by incorporating artist talks and theater into his institution's curriculum. His commitment was expressed this way: "The spirit and language of the visual arts are opened up to man only if he deals with his work in a purposeful, devoted and enduring way; out of the wholeness of his soul" (Schohaus, 1963, pp. 30–31). One of his students, Jakob Hartman, noted how Schohaus showed him a way to fine art, that he learned from him how it is never to be degraded to a mere value object and that the art should be incorporated into life to illuminate the viewer's path (1962 Yearbook, p. 27). Art was part of the atmosphere of Schohaus's classrooms with ever-changing pictures by contemporary artists hanging on the walls. Anton Bernhardsgrütter and Cornelia Forster were just two of the artists whom Schohaus personally knew and supported (A. Engeli, 2018, personal communication).

Schohaus was interested in the quality of his students' lives, perhaps to a fault. For example, a seminarian in Kreuzlingen who was a student of Schohaus from

1956 to 1961 recalled that he was known for holding a contest where he visited students' seminary living quarters to gauge how they kept their rooms: he observed what pictures and decoration were on the walls, what flowers were in what vases, and so on and then rated them, with an award going to the students whose room was finest (Züst, personal communication). His plea for aesthetic education was a hallmark of his pedagogy (A. Engeli, personal communication, March 9, 2018). He further enhanced his aesthetic bona fides by his serving as long-standing secretary of the Lucerna Foundation, an arts-based Swiss grant maker (Bolligen, newspaper article).

Schohaus inculcated a reverence for the natural environment through camping, hikes, and ski trips. Moreover, he maintained and promoted a firm reverence and respect for the nurturance of a child's growth and development through the instincts and guidance of the mother[6] and father and the life of the family. Throughout his career, Schohaus used many outlets for his ideas besides the classroom to reach parents and a more general population. He wrote articles for magazines and newspapers and published "Beauty in Everyday Life" in the *Bischofzeller Zeitung* (a local newspaper) in serial form in 1948. For one particular magazine, *Basler Versicherun*, he contributed a large series of studies with such basicity and clarity on the everyday issue of education, with titles "Homework and Leisure", "Parental Home and School", "Hobbies-Educational", "Your Child Needs Encouragement!", "Blessing and Blessing of Sport", and "Education for the Love of Nature" (Schmid, 1962, p. 35).

Schohaus's position vis-à-vis religion in the curriculum was nuanced. Although he was a proponent of the removal of religious education from the school curriculum, and stirred local controversy among the clergy over this matter, he instituted a time for students to discuss world religions to foster a more widely held regard and reverence for the spiritual life. Schohaus created no pedagogical dogmatics, though. His aim was to humanize education, most clearly expressed in two basic insights in his essay "Turnen und Sport im Rahmen der Gesamterziehung" Gymnastics and Sport in the Framework of Education , where he wrote, Education to humanity is receptive to the wholeness of human-spiritual existence, and the other, education is therefore also the formation of the wholeness of the being to be formed (Schmid, 1962).

Schohaus believed in the value of the teacher and students being self-organized and autonomous. In his view the goal of education is to empower people to fulfill their individual life mission. "Become who you are", as Pindar is quoted. The individual child should be the focus (A. Engeli, personal communication). To these ends, Schohaus instituted student self-governance as an enduring fixture of his tenure as Lehrerseminar director. The principles of living together—getting to know each student, the students getting to know him, spending casual time together, solving problems, and learning to live life collaboratively—were part of the natural *gemeinschaft* or community instinct Schohaus sought to cultivate in his writing, life, and teaching. The teacher should be a vital person who has a hundredfold connection to life and can create fellowship. Children need guidance, but also encouragement (A. Engeli, personal communication). Schohaus wanted the teacher to see the educational situation as a whole in the fundamental, psychological, and personal problematic, and yet keep faith in themselves and in their profession (Schmid, 1962, p. 33).

Schohaus's classroom lectures[7] and educational philosophy ranged from the lyrical poets to the precepts of the New Era progressive educational movement which he grounded in humanistic teaching. "When I think of the lessons by Schohaus", according to one seminarian, "I see in front of me his seated figure at the front desk, his friendly big eyes expressing sympathy for us students, hear his calm, sure voice". Schohaus foregrounded the questions that he asked his students with care for their development: "The questions to us were not just queries, but expressed an interest in our thinking, loosened up by humorous recited anecdotes" (A. Engeli, personal communication, March 9, 2018). According to Schohaus, what is an interesting lesson?

> Every material is interesting which the student can attach organically to previous experience and knowledge. The atmosphere of the lesson is important, which must not only be mental training, but also education of the heart. It should vibrate at school; not as empty straw be threshed. Self-development, practical actions and excursions can make the school more realistic, contributing to the community and making experiences possible.
>
> (A. Engeli, personal correspondence)

Relating this pedagogical approach to discipline, Schohaus believed as a teacher one should be strict and demanding, but this is only justified insofar as the conscience of the pupil properly understood would demand it. It is important to support the still weak conscience. Friz Steinman, a former seminarian (1955–1959), remembered that if a student had been in discussion for insufficient academic performance or for disciplinary reasons, Schohaus would have opened the discussion with the sentence "Gentleman, first the good" (F. Steinman, personal communication). He placed little emphasis on methodological and didactic armor, uniform rigidity for a precise way to teach. The personality of the teacher with a humane attitude was crucial for Schohaus. His way of teaching and his personal sympathy for students were the valued and reliable characteristics (K. Kohli, personal communication, March 10, 2018). Schohaus understood the challenging discipline problems and did not place blame solely on the student:

> Troublemakers are not to be considered sinners, they do not disturb us, they do allow us to understand where educational help is needed if we ask ourselves the question, "Why are they troublemakers?" Sometimes the amazed look is enough: "Please, you're probably not quite in the picture that we're working now." But it can also be due to our lessons. If the students are bored.
>
> (A. Engeli, personal communication, March 9, 2018)

Schohaus's arguments against homework cut against traditional schooling of the time. He stated that

> homework helps many, especially the weak, to lose their school spirit. If possible, the children outside the school should not be bothered with it. They are entitled to leisure, which is often an important source of experiences. Homework can be provided as voluntary and individual exercise, for example, memorizing poems is a worthy after-school endeavor.
>
> (R. Züst, personal communication)

Finally, Schohaus's thoughts on technology still ring true today. A questionable form of progress for civilization, for example, the "Ölgötz" (the television), today often occupies the former place of the nursery. Radio and television can lead to passivity and paralyze the creative genius (A. Engeli, personal communication). No doubt, they are the antithesis to our hoped-for post-pandemic model of schooling. Although the benefits of using technology as a ways and means of schooling are obvious, its dominant role has denigrated and replaced the human touch.

Publication of *Shadow over the School*

Two years after publication of the three-issue exposé in the *Schweizer-Spiegel* in 1930, the results of the survey with commentary were published in book form in Zurich, as *Schatten über der Schule: eine kritische Betrachtung* (*Shadow over the School: A Critical Review*). George Allen & Unwin in London translated the text into English and published it as *The Dark Places of Education: With a Collection of Seventy-Eight Reports of School Experiences* (1932). Careful consideration was given to the educational merits of the text prior to its translated publication. M. M. Mackenzie, a reader of the original German text, in a review note to the publisher and editor, advised:

> This book as it stands in its original form is one of the most excellently expressed and most accurate criticisms of modern education that has yet found publication in any country and is one that ought to be read not only for superficial interest, but studied with profound attention by the laity and members of the educational profession throughout the civilized world.
>
> (Mackenzie, 1931)

Mackenzie further recommended that it was strategic to consider the affiliations and backgrounds of the translator as well as the author of the foreword. The English publisher selected progressive educator Mary Chadwick,[8] an associate member of the British Psychoanalytic Society, as the translator.

P. B. Ballard, author of numerous progressive education texts, including *The Practical Infant Teacher Volumes 1-5* (1935) and *The Changing School* (1926), wrote the foreword, where he exhorts English readers to

Make no mistake about it; the dark places here described do not merely exist in a far-off land: they are here in the schools and homes of England—here in the same number, of the same kind, and with the same degrees of darkness.... These pages are worth reading over and over again; for they illumine the dark places and set before us an ideal of education which is at once noble, inspiring and humane. There is no pettiness: no carping at imaginary ills, no vulgar abuse of any class or section of the community, but a kindly probing of the maladies of our educational systems and a clear pointing of the way to happiness and health.

(pp. 7–8)

With the initial German publication, the term "Schatten über der Schule" (*The Shadow Hanging over the School*) became prevalent as a school reform slogan in Switzerland. Favorable newspaper reviews heralded many of the New Era education values. There were also those who condemned the text as overly critical. Hans Zuliiger, a Swiss educator who applied psychoanalytic practices to children, compared the text to the guilty pleasure of eating strawberry cake, getting painful answers in such large quantities.[9] In the *Neue Zurcher Zeitung* (*New Zurich Times*) on June 16, 1930, the reviewer praised the book, saying it was of inestimable value and offered facts which showed clearer than any pedagogical theory where the problems are in the school system.[10] Yet, in the same newspaper about a week later (June 25, 1930), another reviewer noted that the situations presented in the text are "long ago" examples that are no longer relevant.[11] *Deutsche Rundschau*, an influential conservative literary publication out of Berlin, also reviewed *Schatten über der Schule*. This reviewer noted the relevance in bringing new school practices and ideas to the mass of public schooling, making the text required reading to identify the illnesses in the schools and heal them.[12]

Translation into English and publication of *The Dark Places of Education* took place just prior to the New Era New Education Fellowship Conference held in Nice, France, in 1932, which Schohaus attended along with Montessori, Piaget, and other prominent educators from around the world. In a review in the NEF journal it was noted, "This book is dynamic and therefore worth the attention of people who are alive in the true sense". W. H. Auden, the English poet known fittingly for his early leanings toward Freud and Jung, with his analytical clarity and incisive wit, weighed in on *The Dark Places of Education* in *The Criterion*, a British Literary magazine, in 1933. According to the young Auden,

It is typical of a topsy-turvy way of doing things, that while the pupils in our training colleges are taught child psychology, they learn nothing about their own selves, are given no insight whatsoever into themselves, which in a profession where adults are expected, perhaps inevitably, to profess official opinions on every subject of importance, to lead the private life of a clergyman, where a mask is essential, sets up a strain that only the long holidays of which other professions are often so jealous, safeguard from developing into nervous breakdowns. *The Dark Places of Education* should help the public teaching profession to realize the necessity of lightening these psychological burdens as much as possible, or at least equipping masters and mistresses with the knowledge of how best to bear them.

(Auden, 1996, p. 35)

The English text includes a 100-page introduction by Schohaus followed by 78 narratives/depositions or confessions, as they can be considered, categorized into themes as part of a report on the Swiss education system. If we call the participants' narratives *confessions*, in this context, then they fit into the modern Humanistic *Lebenskunde* methodology of which Schohaus was a forerunner, by including the exact written testimony of the people who respond to his question as the actual text of the book. *Lebenskunde*, or life education, as described by the Humanistischer Verband Deutschlands n.d. (the German Humanistic Association, n.d.), should lead people to understand the importance of moral action and in particular help them to develop moral positions for their own lives and for people to see themselves as members of a vast human community that spans cultures, traditions, and nations.

In choosing to publish the confessionals in the December 1927 Christmas issue of the *Schweizer-Spiegel*, Schohaus and his editor were particularly clever in using the spirit of the season to do exactly this with their readers. The confessionals were a reminder of the dark places in the winter of education, the difficulties and challenges, and the destructive nature; the pernicious good intentions of school policies, practices, and people. In line with the precepts outlined by the NEF, Schohaus placed the dignity of the individual respondent/confessor at the center of readers' thoughts, along with hope and the change sought through compassion evident at this time of year across Judeo-Christian religions. Schohaus was aware of the age-old and recurring problems associated with organized religion. As a Christian and a humanist, with *Schatten über der Schule*, he sought to help people overcome their real conflicts—the struggles placed on people by the realm and workings of schools and schooling—ameliorate their suffering, and further justify the enduring social relationships we have with the institution of school, no matter how challenging. The justification of the ongoing relationship comes in the call for others to understand and work toward reform and improvement of the conditions in schools that causes suffering. It is ironic that Schohaus's book became popular in the German-speaking world and was translated to English during the 1930s, a time when the Nazi regime was powerful. At the NEF conference in Nice in 1932, a new statement of principles had been worked out and introduced that replaced the 1921 version noted above, and was more precise in its awareness of the threat to free peoples everywhere:

In twenty years education might transform the social order and establish a spirit of co-operation capable of finding solutions for the problems of our time.... It is only an education which realizes a change of attitude to children ... that can inaugurate an era free from the ruinous rivalries, the prejudices, anxieties and distress characteristic of our present chaotic insecure civilization.

(Stewart, 1968, p. 226)

1. Education should equip us to understand the complexities of modern social and economic life, safeguarding freedom of discussion by the development of the scientific spirit.

2. It should make adequate provision for meeting diverse intellectual and emotional needs of different individuals, and should afford constant opportunity for active self-expression.

3. It should help us adjust ourselves voluntarily to social requirements, replacing the discipline of fear and punishment by the development of intelligent initiative and independent judgement.

4. It should promote collaboration between all members of the community. This is only possible where teachers are taught alike and understand the value of diversity of character and independent judgement.

5. It should help us to appreciate our own national heritage and to welcome the unique contribution that every other national group can make to the culture of the world. The creation of world citizens is as important for the safety of modern civilization as the creation of national citizens. (*The New Era*, June 1932)

These principles show how acutely aware and committed Schohaus was to the ethical consequences of human decisions in the lives of schoolchildren at a dark turning point in history.

Themes of Suffering in *The Dark Places of Education*

Part one of *The Dark Places of Education* is titled: "Diagnosis: What is wrong with our schools?" In the first two chapters, titled "Daemons" and "Sufferings" respectively, Schohaus sketched out his argument and his analysis of contemporary schooling. The title "Daemons"—meaning "force of nature"—was appropriately chosen, and demands some consideration in light of the present text and the possibility that the daemons Schohaus sought to reveal address common aspects of schooling long taken for granted, daemons that he also sought to exorcise. In many cases, such daemons still exist in our day:

> It would seem to be a law of life that our organizations may become *daemons,* evil spirits against which we must exert ourselves in order to protect our liberty. Otherwise the means will be magnified until it becomes an *end* in itself; the instrument will exist for itself alone, and the creature will at last threaten to overpower its creator.
>
> (Schohaus, 2012/1932, p. 26)

Each of the 78 narratives/confessionals is organized into 13 different themes, all in answer to the question "From what did you suffer most in school?" The themes identified as the topics of the causes of suffering in school were *humanity, corporal punishment, intellectualism, discipline, comradeship, partiality or prejudice toward students, rights of personality, pleasure in achievement, mockery, contempt and sarcasm, provisional life, mis-education, expenditure and results, and the fight against defiance.* The largest number of confessions was categorized as *humanity*, and these emanate from the dichotomy between Schohaus's ideal qualities of teachers and the way students suffered at their shortcomings, whether intentional or unintentional. Schohaus (2012/1932) noted, "The profession of education demands unusual psychological qualities. The backbone of a teacher's character should be comprised of three cardinal virtues: wisdom, goodness and happiness" (p. 81). Exactly how we, and Schohaus, define these virtues are instructional and revealing. A short, concise definition of wisdom, according to Schohaus:

> *Wisdom* does not mean an inexhaustible fund of school learning, not being replete with general education, but possessing a free capacity to form judgements and a sure intuition respecting the essentials and worth of things.
>
> (p. 81)

Schohaus, though, devoted more time and space in defining *goodness*. He clarified the virtuous dispositions of professional pedagogical practice for an important, critical reason—a reminder how, by understanding the suffering narratives, the reader sees how their values have become corrupted.

> Goodness in the educational sense has nothing to do with boring piety, weakness and sentimentality. Goodness is a characteristic which arises from forgetting oneself out of sympathy with the psychological development of another. Goodness of this kind arises from a fundamental reality of character, and a very strong cultural externalisation of personal interests. It is based upon maturity which means well developed mental freedom. It is to be found in persons whose development is constantly active and who, moreover, are as free as possible from their own complexes (fixated subjective inhibitions).
>
> (Schohaus, p. 82, 2012/1932)

Schohaus made goodness, as quality of character, visible through his definition for educators. Serving others' growth by setting aside one's own needs but sharing interests—this is the hallmark of goodness for the educator. We see here a side of Schohaus that is dedicated, also, to speaking to parents. He provided a definition that a mother or father can easily understand. An *externalization of personal interests* means being involved and interested in life, in hobbies, in activities like sports, music, and crafts, and bringing it into the home, classroom or community where they can be shared with children and students. This foreshadows Thomas Merton's guidelines for a robust life, which

> consists in learning to live on one's own, spontaneous, freewheeling: to do this one must recognize what is one's own—be familiar and at home with oneself. This means basically learning who one is, and learning what one

has to offer to the contemporary world, and then learning how to make that offering valid.

(1979, p. 3)

According to Schohaus, the habit or ritual and practice of goodness coincides with that of happiness:

> Happiness is a condition of mature stability in relation to opposing forces of life. It means not taking one's personality too seriously, nor the hardships which come upon us either from without or within. Happiness is compatible with the deepest ethical seriousness and indeed cannot be imagined without it. The right kind of goodness provides warmth of a flourishing educational climate, and happiness its light.

(2012/1932, p. 82)

The narratives that Schohaus categorized into the theme of humanity as a cause of suffering portray educators lacking the virtues of goodness, happiness, and wisdom in their relations with students. The confessions show educators to be inhumane, uncaring, factually oriented, and even brutal: their methods are the cause of great anxiety, embarrassment, and humiliation. As one former student put it, "I suffered most at school from the fact that I was not regarded as a human being and was despised as a pupil" (p. 222). Often students and outside observers accuse teachers of not serving as guides for students in deep personal matters. A recurring notion was that of students not being directly taught about sexuality and the problems of puberty. Another former pupil complained of "being 23 years old and still not knowing where babies come from" (p. 225). This humane call, to alleviate suffering, is through the courageous schoolmaster serving as someone with gentle tact and discernment, providing the soft guidance necessary on the "glorious beauty" of the most sensitive and common of matters (Figure 2.5).

Conclusion

Schohaus's work provides us a blueprint with which we can discern, understand, and alleviate suffering in schools. Although the text is now almost 100 years old, the responses to the question "From what did you suffer most in school?" remain relevant today. Schooling and its educational practices will very well continue to be contentious and vehement into the future, which is a conundrum due to schooling's authoritarian attributes, on the one hand with its focus on compliance, rule boundedness and strict operations, and its demand to motivate, inform, inspire, and enlighten, on the other. It also holds true that when one egregious form of systemic injustice is eliminated, previously overlooked injustices become visible (Levinson, 2015). These systemic injustices—our *daemons*—such as corporal punishment, standardized testing regimes, unequal race-based opportunities, and other practices that stifle individuality and creativity and normalize compliance and submission, have not yet been eradicated

Figure 2.5 Photo of Willi Schohaus in 1967 (photo by Hans Baumgartner).

Source: Thurgauer Jahrbuch (Thurgau Annual)

in schools. New forms and therefore new *daemons* emerge, as school shootings, cyberbullying, and the challenges of teaching and learning in a post-pandemic world illustrate.

The brutal, harsh, and debilitating aspects of education remain stubbornly difficult to exorcise. The problems are systemic ones inherent to the institution itself and how schools operate. Teachers in traditional schools have long had to comply with poor conditions and what they saw as wrong-headed mandates and rules governing their work—implementing teaching strategies or behavior-management programs that do not best serve students (Schwartz, 2019). In our work we have seen teachers reject "innovation funds" or money available to experiment with new methods with the excuse that they simply do not have the time or do not want to face the challenge of creating something new beyond what has been handed to them to deliver. The thought is that it's easier to just play along and conform to the culture evident in one's surroundings. We have also witnessed the same where teachers and their purported leadership live by the maxim, "Keep it simple, stupid". John Dewey insightfully noted that "the school system which makes no great demands upon originality, upon invention, upon the continuous expression of individuality works seemingly automatically to place and keep the more incompetent in the school" (1903). In the chapters that follow we apply

Schohaus's perennial question, "From what did you suffer most in school?" to the contemporary U.S. context. The acts we see perpetrated on children at the expense of the school cause moral injury all around, and a remedy is not easily found nor administered. Progressive, unorthodox, innovative, radical, caring educators have always seen and acted against the dark side of education and worked to eradicate and alleviate the pernicious good intentions evident in school. Creative compliance, resistance [thought criminality], vigilant compassion, and informed and active empathy on the part of teachers, administrators, school workers, and researchers are all necessary as we work to create an institution that clarifies and improves the social, emotional, academic, and moral lives of its members.

Notes

1 This is from a review of *Schatten uber dur Schule* in *The Swiss Teacher's Newspaper* "Schweizerische Lehrerzeitung" in 1931 under the editorship of Dr. Walter Klauser. Gerhard Fricke compiled an extensive collection of Swiss reviews of Schohaus's text in the 2000–2001 *Kreuzlingen Teacher Seminar Yearbook*.

2 "Worunter haben Sie in der schule am moisten meisten? gelitten?" This article by Schohaus appeared in 1927 in *Schweizer-Spiegel* [*The Swiss Mirror*]. *The Swiss Mirror* was published by childhood friend of Schohaus, A. Gugenbuhl. It had a circulation of approximately 12,000 at the time of publication.

3 This fact is noted in English language reviews of the translated text including: Author Unknown (1932, December 31) Advertiser, Adelaide South Australia: (1932, November 1) *The Expository Times* vol. 44, 2: pp. 66-67.

4 Paul Häbelin (1878–1960) studied theology and philosophy, and had a background in the natural sciences—botany and zoology.

5 See R. Isler's discussion in *Jahre Stabilität und innovation-die Thurgauer Lehrerbildung und ihre Gebaude* (2008, p. 175). Here the roots of Schohaus's philosophy of education pertain to the influence of Zarathustran ideas.

6 Schohaus had columns that appeared in *Schweizer-Spiegel* from time to time, titled "Frau und Haushalt" or The Wife/Woman/Mrs. and the Home," which addressed timely, progressive perspectives on common parenting issues. One from the December 1937 issue was titled *Weihnachts geschenke sind keine Belohnungen* or "Christmas gifts are not rewards".

7 The notes that follow are from the personal notebooks, translated from German, of Arne Engeli, a seminarian in Kreuzlingen 1951–1955.

8 Mary Chadwick (?–1943), Associate member of the British Psychoanalytic Society and member of the New Era education progressives. She received her psychoanalytic training and was a lecturer at the British College of Nurses. She published numerous works in English and German on the psychology of children and education, including: *Die Gott-Phantasie bei Kindern*, 1927, *Difficulties in Child Development*, London, 1928. *The Psychological Effects of Menstruation*, New York, Washington 1932. *Adolescent Girlhood*. New York 1932.

9 The reviews discussed here originally in German are compiled from a translated version of a biography of Willi Schohaus written by Gerhard Fricke titled: *Willi Schohaus. Erziehung durch Ermutigung und mit Autorität (Jahreshefte der Ehemaligen des Seminars Kreuzlingen 2000/2001)* [*Willi Schohaus. Education Through Encouragement and with Authority*] (Yearbook of the Kreuzlingen Teacher Seminar 2000–2001).

10 Ibid.

11 Ibid.

12 Ibid.

References

Auden, W.H. (1996). *Prose and travel books in prose and verse.* Princeton University Press.

Haenggeli-Jenni, B. (2016). «New Education», *Encyclopédie pour une histoire nouvelle de l'Europe*[online], published 06/09/2016, consulted 29/10/2018. http://ehne.fr/en/node/793

Brehony, K.J. (2006). Early years education: some Froebelian contributions. *History of Education, 35*(2), 167–172. https://doi.org/10.1080/00467600500528016

Dewey, J. (1903). Democracy in education. *The Elementary School Teacher, 4*(4), 193–204.

Frick, G. (1962). For the 80th Birthday of Willi Schohaus (translated from German) *Jahresheft der Altgymnastika und der hemaligen des seminars Kreuzlingen.* (Yearbook of the Kreuzlingen Teacher Seminar) G. Frick, Ed. M. Grob, Amriswil.

Humanistischer Verband Deutschlands. (n.d.). Humanism—for the sake of reason and humanity. *HVD-hessen.* https://www.hvd-hessen.de/english/

Isler, R. (2008). *175 jahre stabillat und innovation-Die thurgauer Lehrerbildung und ihre Gebaude.* [175 years of stability and innovation-the Thurgau teacher education and its buildings]. PH Thurgau Festschrift.

Kobi, E. E. (1981, June 27, 28e). Zum Gedenken an Willi Schohaus [In Memory of Willi Schohaus]. *Neue Zircher Zeitung,* p. 36.

Grunder, H.-U. (2011). "New schools", in: *Historical Dictionary of Switzerland (DHS)* , version dated 05.10.2011, translated from German. Online: https://hls-dhs-dss.ch/fr/articles/010413/2011-10-05/, consulted on 20.04.2022.

Hofstetter, R., & Schneuwly, B. (2006). Progressive education and educational sciences: The tumultuous relations of an indissociable and irreconcilable couple? (late 19th–mid 20th century). In R. Hofstetter & B. Schneuwly (Eds.), *Passion, fusion, tension: New education and educational sciences: End 19th–middle 20th century* (pp. 1–16). Peter Lang.

Kinchin, J. (1999). The new school. In J. Kinchin & A. O'Connor (Eds.), *The century of the child: Growing by design* (pp. 99–103). The Museum of Modern Art.

Levinson, M. (2015) Moral injury and the ethics of educational injustice. *Harvard Educational Review, 85*(2), 203–228.

Merton, T. (1979). *Love and living.* Harcourt Books.

Reader's report by an unidentified reader[M. MacKenzie] on Schatten uber der Schule / by Willi Schohaus (1931). Reference Aurr 5/7/24 Ascension number- ms 3282 Museum of English Rural Life, Special Collections Service, University of Reading, Great Britain.

Reese, W. J. (2001) The origins of progressive education. *History of Education Quarterly, 14*(1).

Schmid, J. (1962). Zum Geist der pädagogische Schriften von Willi Schohaus. In Frick G., Jahresheft der Altgymnastika und der Ehemaligen des Seminars Kreuzlingen. Max Grob.

Schohaus, W. (1927a, October). Worunter haben Sie in der schule am moisten gelitten? [From what did you suffer most in school?] *Swiss Mirror/Schweizer-Spiegel*

Schohaus, W. (1927b). *Pestalozzis Werke Säkularausgabe in Drei Bänden Komplett: Ausgewahlt und Herausgegeben von Willi Schohaus.* [Pestalozzi's works secular edition in three volumes complete: Selected and edited by Willi Schohaus] Leopold Klotz Gotha

Schohaus, W. (2012/1932). *The dark places of education: with a collection of 78 reports of school experiences.* (M. Chadwick, Trans.). Routledge.

Schohaus, W. (1963). *Erziehung zur Menschlichkeit.* [Education for humanity]. Huber.

Soëtard, M. (1994). Jean-Jacques Rousseau (1712-78). *PROSPECTS: Quarterly Review of Comparative Education.* vol. XXIV, no. 3/4, pp. 423–438.

Stewart, W.A.C. (1968). *The educational innovators: volume 2 progressive schools 1881-1967.* Macmillan.

Trohler, D. (2001). Johann Heinrich Pestalozzi 1746-1827. In J.A. Palmer, & L. Bresler & D.E. Cooper (Eds.) *Fifty major thinkers on education.* (pp. 64–69). Routledge.

3 Understanding Suffering for Educators

The art of happiness is the art of suffering well.

(Hahn, 2014)

This chapter is a review of the literature on suffering. We draw from medicine, psychology, social sciences, religion, and education to bring many threads of thinking about suffering together. In doing so, we hope to build a dialectical bridge and further formulate a working definition that helps school leaders frame a comprehensive gestalt and enable them to better understand, respond to, and alleviate suffering of students in schools. We aim to broaden an imaginative appreciation and related dispositions by which school leaders encounter others as whole persons and function more responsively in their day-to-day work.

Physicians, nurses, psychologists, social scientists, philosophers, and other caring professionals all labor to alleviate suffering and comfort the human condition in their own particular way and from their own particular vantages. Learning these fundamental professional perspectives on suffering may henceforth further aid educators as they attempt to nurture students and provide a means to persist and flourish through challenges and afflictions brought on by school-related hardships. School leaders serve in an everyman/woman role and in turn, their audience in local communities is the general public itself. The day-to-day interactions and the administrative decisions they make impact the lives of students and families in myriad ways. School administrators must adapt, relate, and respond humanely to a new collective consciousness evident by the tumultuous second decade of the 21st century. The global coronavirus pandemic as well as the changed, permanent climate of ongoing disruptive domestic political issues arising from the George Floyd murder, the January 6, 2021 attack on the U.S. Capitol, and the ever-increasingly salient global challenges in facing the realities of a warming planet all contribute to large-scale social realities that have a detrimental impact on communities, students, families, and their schools. Individual and group emotional distress, shared and isolated global grief, racial inequality, the impact of social distancing, and compressed remote learning are just a few of the larger issues impacting schools directly and indirectly that leaders must adjust to and contend with. The larger ecology in which schools operate is one that is conducive to the more immediately proximate suffering experienced by students in schools.

DOI: 10.4324/9780429465499-3

Although this literature review is not exhaustive, it is wide-ranging in our aim to expand the parameters of useful knowledge and insights into the phenomenon of suffering in schools. One goal here is to foster educator vision that further elucidates teacher and school leader mission-driven goals, dispositions, and behaviors that contribute to their further formation as caring and empathetic professionals. We ask our readers to contemplate foundational human conditions they may have not explicitly considered before or applied in their cognitive, social, professional, imaginative, and emotional frameworks for understanding their work in schools. We also want to encourage attention to different domains within a school leader's own educational transcripts—reflecting on and furthering their understanding of other fields like medicine, psychology and spirituality in ways not previously applied in PK–12 school realms.

We are not denying the helpful and compassionate work school administrators and educators already do. An ethic of care (Noddings, 2010) in service to the best interests of a student (Stefkovich & Frick, 2021) is crucial to school administrators as a matter of moral motivation and professional integrity. Every person involved in the schooling process deserves to be treated with dignity and respect (Normore & Jarrett, 2021; Sporre, 2020; Ronay, 2019; Hantzopolous, 2016). Yet, students everywhere still suffer due to the pernicious good intentions of education practices, policies, and people who work in schools. The difficulty of school leadership in an age of global educational reform, where accountability is valued over responsibility, presents substantial quandaries in managing roles that are multifaceted and incorporate care, concern, and connection alongside academic rigor (Sahlberg, 2012; Louis et al., 2016). The conditions of life that school age children and teens must respond to have changed. In a phrase, it can be brutal out there. Suffering contains a special call to the practice of virtue, and those who labor in this domain make considering the pain of others a daily occurrence (Cassidy, 2010).

Medicine

The discussion here will use the more encompassing term "clinician" in reference to health care professionals who provide direct care to a patient. This includes physicians, nurses, practicing psychologists, and other medical team members besides those working in administration or research. Following this section, there will be a focused discussion on the religious, psychological, and educational approaches to understanding and alleviating suffering.

The medical clinician must consider that any state of health or medical occurrence may give rise to suffering. The relevance of acknowledging the transition from a state of health to a state of illness requires an experiential and existential change in the way we perceive humanity (Pellegrino, 1995). Understanding of medical science is a component of the foundation of traditional caring. Clinicians do not solely treat a disease. A disease is an affliction of the whole person, and not just the body (Cassell, 1999, 2004). The same disease in diverse patients presents itself differently due to individual and group variances such as genetics;

anatomical make-up; and social, educational, and economic stability. The intent to manage and alleviate suffering requires a practitioner to invest in a therapeutic relationship with a patient to establish trust and confidence. The compassionate and competent clinician strives to connect with the patient in this fashion.

Pellegrino and Gray's (1994) theory of medicine and the healing relationship establishes medicine and nursing as particular types of human activity that include three parts: *the fact of illness, the act of profession,* and *the act of medicine.* The *fact of illness* is the person moving from a state of health to illness once realizing something is wrong physically or psychologically and they seek help from a physician. This person is anxious and vulnerable, and they may have lost some element of their practical autonomy. The *act of the profession* begins when the clinician asks, "How may I help you?" and requires the knowledge learned and needed to help and to heal the patient. The *act of healing* may be described as a diagnostic, prognostic, and therapeutic act—one that utilizes manipulation, judgment, cognition, and prescription directed at what is necessary to heal and help an individual.

The practice of medicine maintains a reliance on two models of prevailing thought when treating patients: the biomedical and the biopsychosocial. Biomedical, external sources such as viruses, germs, and bacteria and physical sources like genetic predispositions and chemical imbalances are the causes of illness (Cockerham, 2021; Bemme & Kirmayer, 2020; Engebretsen, 2018; Cantor, 2000). In the biomedical model, the illness is beyond the patient's control. Treatment is by vaccination, surgery, medicine, chemotherapy, etc. In the biopsychosocial model, biological, psychological, and social factors play a role in the context of understanding and curing the disease (Aftab & Nielsen, 2021; Engel, 1977). A person is ultimately cured using a multifaceted medicinal, social, and therapeutic approach that addresses changes in behavior, beliefs, coping strategies, and medical treatment (Farre & Rapley, 2017). It is the incorporation of approaches that encompasses a focus on the individual to establish a treatment that might cure or help manage the future risks of the illness.

Medical personnel are trained to make decisions based on factual, objective, observations in identifying what is wrong with a patient's body, and also understanding the subjective nature of the individual person who is suffering (Cho et al., 2021; Cassell, 1999). Why and how a person is suffering in the way they are is subjective, unique, and personal and must be considered in diagnosis and treatment. Although the scientific biomedical language a doctor uses to describe a disease is quite different from the individual patient's narrative of their ailments, a biopsychosocial approach aims at bridging the gap (Cho et al., 2021; Cassell, 1999). Charon (2017) noted the affective and creative parts of medical training and experience bring about powerful emotions such as rage, love, helplessness, power, and ecstasy. The embodiment and processing of these challenging emotions occur in the line of duty when they are experienced by the caring professional and develop into helpful, gentle, and considerate relationships with real people (Charon, 2017).

Suffering impacts the composition of a person's life and may bring about a sense of alienation. When one is suffering due to a physical or mental illness, they may lose the ability to fulfill intentions and obligations on deep personal and social levels. Suffering fosters the loss of acceptable meaning, and any nourishment provided by personal connection may be compromised (Younas, 2020; Johnston, 2013; Reich, 1989). Lives become uncontrollable when there is a feeling of helplessness and the psychosocial and personal resources for coping can become depleted because of this. Biomedically, a patient relies on a clinician for proper care to manage pain, but treatment of the disease is only part of the alleviation of suffering. There is criticism though of the way in which the biomedical model can depersonalize the most personal and intimate struggles through the use of myriad methodologies, clinical remedies, techniques, and strategies (Double, 2021; Fowers et al., 2017; Davies, 2012). Biopsychosocially, alleviating suffering demands the understanding of a patient's social, emotional, physical, and contextual response to their ailments. Suffering as a *feeling*, rather than objective analysis of physical state, demands a hermeneutical assessment of the holistic interior landscape of a patient.

No cure will last without care, nor will care alone be successful in curing a person (Elias, 1990). An act of compassion involves recognizing a specific negative emotional state (like pain) and then seeking to help that person (Weisz & Zaki, 2017). Although empathy as a practice is understood as a cognitive, emotional, and communication skill, it is truly composed of a clinician's ability to care, worry about, communicate, and understand the experience their patient is going through in a vicarious way (Citra et al., 2021). Empathetic attunement or empathic attentiveness is developed by deeply understanding the emotional, phenomenal, and sociocultural world their patient inhabits (Glucksman, 2020; Stiegler et al., 2018; Chapman & Gavrin, 1993; Cassell, 1999). Empathy reveals itself in the clinician's practice through a number of clearly visible ways, such as in their diagnostic accuracy, the ability to establish trust with the patient (and loved ones), communicating an understanding of the disease and its ramifications to the patient as well as to other health care professionals working with the patient, and working to increase the patient's satisfaction and quality of life (Citra et al., 2021). Having and showing empathy, like understanding and alleviating suffering, is a complex experiential, cognitive, and emotional phenomenon that requires presence and humanistic awareness. Expertise in the knowledge and treatment of diseases employs the physician's lived experience and informs their discretionary, empathetic, and demonstrative responses to healing their patient.

The alleviation of pain and suffering in a patient with a life-limiting diagnosis is a component of palliative care. It is in the individual perception of the social and emotional impact of pain where a person suffers most. Between life and death, palliative care relieves without necessarily addressing the disease by helping the patient acknowledge their current state of existence. Palliative care prepares for a different version of life where dying is a part of the person's living experience. The sensitive and intimate nature of comforting the dying requires a clinician to understand that a patient's despair cannot be resolved. In addition, the clinician provides tools so that the patient may be protected from demoralization taking hold and invests in preserving of the patient's dignity (F. Mulé, personal communication, July 8, 2021).

The topic of existential distress and its relief in terminal patients is an important one in the understanding of and alleviation of suffering in school-age youth. We propose for later discussion that feelings of ennui, or general dissatisfaction and boredom, that students feel due to modern approaches to schooling, may actually parallel feelings of anxiety and uncertainty patients feel at end of life. Morita et al. (2000) identified existential distress/suffering in terminally ill cancer patients as a multidimensional symptom having 13 categories (Table 3.1).

We see how this list compiles 13 ways that one may suffer *with* but also *without* a life-limiting diagnosis. These 13 categories are instructional for the consideration of the ways in which we suffer in daily life. Existential suffering consists of themes of loneliness, the need to be in the presence of others, and a sense of connectedness. The healing relationship constitutes the clinicians' work, their active healing *presence,* the acknowledgment of shared human vulnerability, and the fulfilling of a longing to end barriers by dissolving distance. Younger (1995) furthered the idea and importance that suffering helps provide meaning by enabling the patient to move from pain to moments of healing and understanding. In addition, the clinician acts out their primary moral role to bind the suffering and non-suffering to the same community (Younger, 1995; Cassidy, 2010; Frank, 2019). Healing existential suffering is complex work; dignity therapy is shown to be promising in this regard (Nunziante et al., 2021; Schuelke & Rubenstein, 2020). The difficulty and

Table 3.1 Categories of Existential Distress

Meaninglessness in present life	expressing one no longer feels any meaning in their present lives
Meaninglessness in past life	expressing one cannot find any meaning in their past lives
Loss of social role functioning	feeling there are no significant roles entrusted to them
Feeling emotionally irrelevant	disclosing feelings that they are neither needed nor loved by anyone
Dependency	stating that a loss of control over self-care or increased dependency is of great concern
Burden on others	grieving they are a nuisance, troubling family members or medical staff
Hopelessness	claiming they cannot look forward to anything or find hope in future
Grief over imminent separation	state they cannot bear impending separation from their loved ones
Why me?	question why they should be suffering
Guilt	consider their disease or suffering is a result of sin or punishment
Unfinished business	worry about goals not achieved or unfilled aspirations
Life after death	have concerns about life after death or death itself
Faith	have concerns related to a specific faith or religion.

nuances of suffering work realize the biopsychosocial model moving beyond the physical whereby psychological, social, spiritual, and existential concerns are considered in the healing relationship.

Providing existential care is one type of suffering work. It incorporates compassion, an acknowledgment of a transcendent possibility and shared human vulnerability of our common fates, and evokes the humanity of the human heart (Cassidy, 2010; Watson, 2005; Campbell 1988). It is the clinician's *presence* that addresses suffering and ultimately heals. A clinician's presence aims to humanize the experience overall and decrease barriers between the doctor, hospital and patient. Asking questions beyond *How may I help you?* such as *Are you suffering? I know you have pain, but are there things that are worse than just the pain? Are you frightened by all this? What exactly are you frightened of? What do you worry (are afraid) is going to happen to you? What is the worst thing about all this?* (Cassell, 1999, p. 532) opens the patient's narrative. Suffering is a paradoxical phenomenon. It arises in a patient through the danger and threats they feel. When a patient is suffering they are in conflict with themselves and how they are trying to relate to their conditions being out of sync with what they see in the world around them. The space, time and freedom patients are given to voice their lament, along with help, understanding and caring from clinicians attuned with their narrative, hopefully leads to a new wholeness that enables the patient to understand their suffering and heal.

Psychology

Trained listeners as they are, psychologists see humanity through a profound, inimitable window. The field of psychology plays an integral part in the biopsychosocial as well as the biomedical method of medical practice and contributes to a substantial role in understanding health and illness as a behavioral health discipline (Wahass, 2005). Psychologists are skilled in areas such as life course development, personality formation, relationships, motivation, how people learn, emotions, cognition, and social factors influencing health and illness. They work independently conducting research, consulting with clients, or working with patients. Others work in the alleviation of suffering as part of a healthcare team, collaborating with physicians and social workers, and they may work in schools, interacting with students, teachers, parents, and other educators. Exerting oneself on the behalf of others' mental health necessitates both compassion and empathy. Doing suffering work intends to improve the quality of people's physical, psychological, and social lives with healthy habits for desirable outcomes that have lasting potential.

Freud (1930) adduced in *Civilization and Its Discontents* that humans are vulnerable to suffering from three directions: our own bodies, the external world, and our relations to other people. Jung noted in the 1933 lecture delivered at Eidgenössische Technische Hochschule Zürich (ETH Zurich)—the "Swiss Federal Institute of Technology Zurich"—that healing the psyche and offering solace, comfort, and salvation to suffering people was historically the prerogative of religion. He proposed that new viewpoints had arisen which see each individual as a whole with their own unique forms of suffering which the field of psychology is capable of addressing (2019). Notably, Schohaus's doctoral thesis was titled *Die Theoretischen Grundlagen und die Wissenschaftstheoretische Stellung der Psychonalysis* [*The Theoretical Foundations and Scientific Theory of Psychoanalysis*] (1923), a clear imprint of the influence Freud and Jung as his contemporaries.

Davies (2012) further elaborated on Freud in *The Importance of Suffering* with an exploration of the value and meaning of suffering and the influence of emotional discontent in our lives. Davies introduced a relational perspective rejecting suffering as simply a mental disorder potentially tied to biology. This viewpoint emphasizes that suffering is a result of the way in which we relate to our external and internal worlds. It is a universal rigidity of maintaining long-held ideas, habits, customs, norms, and beliefs that foster the conditions of suffering. Davies identified six typical scenarios that commonly provoke suffering that warrant our attention and inform our work:

- We suffer to the extent that the conditions to which we are adjusted inhibit the realization of our full potential and the satisfaction of our basic needs. (These conditions can be either oppressive, psychological, or social conditions.).
- We suffer when our defiance of stultifying conditions leads us in to isolation, confusion or a conflicted relationship with our social group.
- We suffer when we successfully anesthetize the pain of being adapted to oppressive conditions (social or psychological) by the use of drugs, delusions, and escapist activities.
- We suffer when our internalized habits fall out of step with our environment. This may be due to a shift in the external environment (social upheaval, loss of someone we love, getting promoted) or shift internal environment (our values shift, we encounter new parts of ourselves).
- We suffer when we fight to change the existing social or psychological conditions into forms that will serve our realizations and of those around us.
- We suffer when we have an inadequate grasp of the causes of suffering (e.g., when we are unaware of the social, political, or psychological factors impeding us). (2012, p. 28).

Davies proposed that our sufferings are not always indicators of being disordered, or ill, but instead that we are emotionally aware; attentive to the conflicts that arise in response to the different positions we can take when navigating social reality. This is what causes one to suffer; it is a realization, not (yet) understood. An education that informs of the causes of suffering, and that suffering is a natural response to external conditions, is an education par excellence which we advocate.

Suffering is hard to overcome alone. An unproductive state of suffering means one is experiencing negative emotions in such a way that they are in depression, remorseful, inactive, static, dependent, and/or constrained. These states of being are due to physical, social, and moral injury due to challenging, unfortunate, and difficult life events, and are part of human processes to better understand circumstances and re-calibrate; but, these should not become permanent states. A psychologist is trained with the ability to identify negative emotional conditions that grounds their facility for a compassionate response, helping others to creatively overcome (Weisz & Zaki, 2017). Söelle correctly stated, "Nothing can be learned from suffering unless it is worked through" (1975, p. 126). Although suffering *is* painful, the most vital aspect of suffering well is being able to eventually use one's distress in a constructive, fruitful way (Corradi-Fiumara, 2015). A sense of perhaps productivity or creativity can move one to an improved state of being that is actively peaceful, more varied, and possibly liberating. We are not speaking about the creativity of art or science, but the creative effort we put into achieving psychic survival, coexistence, and empathy every day (Corradi-Fiumara, 2015). Winnicott proposed the labor of a psychologist, and other caring professionals, is in realizing that within the suffering person is "hidden away somewhere ... a secret life [exists] that is satisfactory because of it being creative or original to that human being" (1971, p. 68). The caring healer, alongside the suffering person, labors to help uncover, reveal, and spark the ever-present creative fire back into the life of their fellow human. In concluding this brief consideration of the literature on approaches to the physician–patient relationship and the alleviation of suffering from a medical and psychological perspective, Pellegrino (1995) listed seven virtues that define the good physician and nurse that begins to offer further insight into dispositional attitudes of the medical profession that are both informative and instructive to the thoughtful and careful educator (Table 3.2).

Additionally, researchers identified and validated seven ideal physician behavior themes that named and defined as follows (Bendapudi et al., 2006) (Table 3.3):

Taken together these virtues and traits constitute a portrait of *vita boni medicus* who practices the art and science of alleviating suffering and ultimately healing

Table 3.2 Virtues of the Medical Practitioner

Fidelity to trust and promise	The inherent and necessary trust between patient and physician.
Benevolence	Every act by the clinicians must be in the patient's interests.
Effacement of self-interest	Protecting patients from vulnerability and exploitation via power, profit, prestige, or pleasure.
Compassion and caring	Open and non-judgmental seeing, hearing, and feeling who others are so as to act in their benefit.
Intellectual honesty	Acknowledging when one does not know something and being humble enough to admit ignorance.
Justice	Justice as a virtue in the healing relationship requires removing the blindfold and adjusting what is owed to the specific needs of the patient, even if those needs do not fit the definition of what is strictly owed.
Prudence	Any clinical decision of note requires prudent weighing of the alternatives in situations of uncertainty and stress

Table 3.3 Ideal Attributes of the Medical Practitioner

Behavior/Sentiment	Description of behavior
Confident	An assured manner engenders trust. The doctor's confidence gives the patient confidence.
Empathetic	Understanding what the patient is feeling and experiencing, physically and emotionally, and communicates that understanding back to the patient.
Humane	Exhibiting care, compassion, and kindness.
Personal	Showing interest in the patient more than just as a patient. Interacts and remembering the patient as an individual.
Forthright	Telling the patient what they need to know in plain language and in a forthright manner.
Respectful	Takes the patient's input seriously and working with their idiosyncrasies.
Thorough	Being both conscientious and persistent.

patients. The professional engaged in the lament of a patient is characterized by their personal, intimate, relational, humanistic care. The work of caring for a suffering person involves recognizing their suffering, sincerely acknowledging it matters, sharing understanding, and finally acknowledging that it is significant (Gleave, 2005). Implications for the work of educators are profound. Central to this is moving from surface awareness to an empathetic attunement of deeply understanding the emotional, phenomenal, and sociocultural world of suffering that many students inhabit.

Religion and Philosophy

Religion involves beliefs, feelings, attitudes, and practices meant to respond to a reality believed to lie beyond our physical world yet causally linked to it (Matthews, 2012). With over 300 religious belief systems worldwide and over 83% of global inhabitants identifying with a religion, faith and spirituality play an important role in the contexts of our lives (Pew Research Center, 2012). In the theological and philosophical traditions of many religions and cultures, the purpose, meaning, and causes of human suffering are central themes. Religious groups, theological schools, and philosophers all grapple with the meaning and alleviation of suffering. In the religious tradition, there are leaders, shamans, pastors, priests, imams, rabbis, members of the clergy, laypersons, and others who provide spiritual, social, and emotional care to members of their religious community. These spiritual caregivers apply theological and philosophical rationales along with kind, compassionate, and empathetic practices and rituals that allow for the contemplation of the nature and universality of suffering in order to help people find solace in its difficult mystery. Through sacred spaces, stories, dances, religious dramas, and sacred writings, each religion interprets the world (Matthews, 2012). These communities of support, consolation, and jubilation provide believers with material for acceptance and understanding of their circumstances. In doing so, a communal and spiritual connection to others is formed—around hardship, affliction, and pain—where we learn how in our suffering, we are not alone. In community, one can more easily accept suffering as part of the dark side of our lives, and the central core religious precepts provide the discipline and reasons to come together and celebrate, nevertheless.

Suffering is a fundamentally negative aspect of our collective human condition. Recognizing this, Levinas (1999) noted that the least one can say about suffering is that in its own phenomenality, intrinsically, it is useless, "for nothing" (p. 157). Yet, acknowledging the void, loss, and pain that suffering causes through a contemplative, religious, spiritual, reflexive praxis aims to bring about understanding and something perhaps useful, or even educative. It is through suffering that we become more aware of our own reality as it strips away the daily habit and routine which anchors us to our existence (Younger, 1995). Since we are finite creatures that suffer illness, death, and one another, suffering is a natural consequence of the beating of life's rhythm (Ekstrom, 2021; Siddiqui, 2021; Starr, 2019; Southgate, 2018; Hauerwas, 2001; Soelle, 1975). It is when suffering is seen as something valuable that it makes spiritual connection and transformation possible (Norris, 2009). Nietzsche (2014) explained that suffering offers humanity a chance to progress toward a higher order of consciousness. Although, without care, concern, connection, and compassion readily available or accessible, suffering through such experiences of pain, despair, social stigma, isolation, anxiety, depression, or fear is simply debilitating, demoralizing, and hopeless.

Possibly the most deliberated question in the history of religion is the cause of human suffering (Perkins, n.d.; Rouzati, 2018; Castelo, 2012; Tilley, 2000). Many have contemplated at one time or another, "If there is a God, and they are beneficent, why is such earthly suffering allowed?" The question of the existence, persistence, and justification of suffering and why it occurs is known as theodicy. Theodicy is the "intellectual defense of God in the face of evil and suffering" (Dein et al., 2013) or, in other words, "the vindication of divine providence in relation to the existence of evil" (The New Shorter Oxford English Dictionary, 1993). Theodicy strikes the grand dissonant chord in the history of humanity; it enables us to realize personal and global sufferings are part of a vast human collectivity. At the most preliminary, basic, and personal levels, the initial subject matter of theodicy is *raw pain* (Farley, 1999 as cited in Confoy, 2000).

For students who hold religious and spiritual perspectives and are suffering, a school leader's knowledge of the broader strokes of the different religious perspectives on suffering will foster a closer relationship and result in more compassionate and empathic understanding in a time of need. This has nothing to do with the separation of religion and the state as a legal issue in the United States and has everything to do with being informed and sensitive to the interests of students (Stefkovich & Frick, 2021). In the reporting below on the religious perspectives on suffering, you will clearly see there are contrary beliefs across the different traditions. Though, as a whole, we hope to inform a caring universal spiritual and charismatic educational leadership disposition.

Christianity

In Christianity, suffering is intimately linked with human corporeal, moral, and spiritual existence and is further revealed and redeemed through Christ's suffering and holy salvation. In Christianity, salvation is achieved through suffering, whether it is one's own or that of Christ (Siddiqui, 2021; Van Hooft, 1998; Etienne, 1995). "Suffering, in fact, is always *a trial*—at times a very hard one—to which humanity is subjected" (John Paul II, 1984, section 23). As presented in the Book of Job, suffering is painful, meaningless, torturous, and may leave one destitute, childless, aimless, wanting, and lost. "While it is true that suffering has a meaning as punishment, when it is connected with a fault, *it is not true* that *all suffering is a consequence of a fault and has the nature of a punishment*" (John Paul II, 1984, section 11). Although people will suffer because of their transgressions as castigation, and repentance is in order, what we learn from Job is that even the innocent suffer (Boyle, 2003; Carmy, n.d.). Elucidated in Job, in whichever way suffering arrives, a Christian identifies and accepts their suffering as redemptive in union with Christ's suffering on the cross. Although suffering is considered negative, when it is given a meaningful context within the larger narrative of humanity, it becomes something positive. By believing and doing so, we are able to maintain and increase our sense of meaning and integration despite trauma (Siddiqui, 2021; Van Hooft, 1998; Etienne, 1995).

William James, the American philosopher, historian, and psychologist, elevated the spiritual, pragmatic, and ecstatic power and central place of the Christian perspective on suffering. What the suffering Christian "craves is to be consoled in his very powerlessness, to feel that the spirit of the universe recognizes and secures him, all decaying and failing as he is" (James, 1902/2012, p. 38). It is impossible to fix the disharmony of suffering, affirming that suffering is a fundamental part of the human condition (Fitzpatrick et al., 2016). And yet, it does not end with mere acceptance; rather, when one is suffering:

> religion comes to our rescue and takes our fate into her hands. There is a state of mind, known to religious men, but to no others, in which the will to assert ourselves and hold our own has been displaced by a willingness to close our mouths and be as nothing in the floods and waterspouts of God. In this state of mind, what we most dreaded has become the habitation of our safety, and the hour of our moral death has turned into our spiritual birthday. The time for tension in our soul is over, and that of happy relaxation, of calm deep breathing, of an eternal present, with no discordant future to be anxious about, has arrived. Fear is not held in abeyance as it is by mere morality, it is positively expunged and washed away.
>
> (James, 1902/2012, p. 14)

In a concluding summary of suffering within Christian traditions, "It is suffering, more than anything else, which clears the way for the grace which transforms human souls" (John Paul II, 1984, section 27).

Judaism

From biblical through modern times, it is said that suffering is at the center of Jewish identity (Benbassa, 2010). A realistic and pragmatic theological vision, Judaism acknowledges the factual belief that evil and suffering exist in the world and that philosophical-speculative thought cannot overcome monstrous evil (Soloveitchik, 1958). In Judaic philosophy, there is the earthly realization that suffering happens and it always will. God is not responsible for it. Although it is not known why suffering exists or occurs, it is believed that God exists within it and it is human action, not God, that will alleviate it. So, the essential question in Judaic thought is not, "Why does suffering and evil exist?" or "Why do I suffer?" but, rather, "What does suffering obligate [humankind] to do?" and "What should the sufferer do to live with [their] suffering?" (Soloveitchik, 1958; Carmy, n.d.).

Zoloth (as cited in Fitzpatrick et al., 2016) noted these questions help present how suffering is viewed—not automatically as a problem of physical being, but one of ethics and how one responds when faced with it. It is not enough to just admit and recognize that suffering exists, that but suffering necessitates human action to alleviate it. Suffering requires as much a social and moral call as it does an existential response as well. This is true of the one suffering, as much as it is true for the one in a position to heal. It is the response to suffering that contains meaning rather than in the understanding of why it has occurred (Dein et al., 2013). Jewish interpretations of suffering rest on the idea that the social welfare, charity, medicine, and science needed to assuage suffering are acts of justice; they are the necessary moral and practical human response to an unjust and as yet unredeemed world (Zoloth, as cited in Fitzpatrick et al., 2016).

Buddhism

Siddhārtha Gautama left his home as a young man and ventured out into the world encountering suffering all around, realizing it to be a fundamental feature of human existence. The mystery of suffering is revealed through Buddhist teachings. The Buddha said, "Suffering I teach, and the Way out of suffering" (Schloegal, 1982, as cited in Austin, 1999, p. 355). Understanding, alleviating, and ultimately *extinguishing* suffering are at the center of Buddhist *dharma*, or philosophy, practice, and teachings. The Four Noble Truths and the Eightfold Path provide a middle pathway [the Middle Way] between asceticism and indulgence for the cessation of suffering and a follower's ultimate enlightenment. The First Noble Truth is *the truth of suffering*: *dukkha* or dis-ease, which translates as suffering that is a part of our everyday existence including the elements of birth, life, aging, and death which all manifest as suffering. The Second Truth is *the causes of suffering*: *samudaya*, which refers to the causes of suffering as constant "craving" or "desiring", the I-me-mine-egocentric conditioning which we cling and attach to for things worldly, material and immaterial alike. The Third Truth—*the cessation of suffering*—refers to the cease from craving or *nirodha* and teaches that desires are innumerable and inexhaustible but one still vows to put an end to them. This state is known as *nirvana,* which translates from Sanskrit to "becoming extinguished" as in putting out the fire of our cravings. The Fourth Truth is *the path that frees us from suffering,* or *magga,* which is known as the middle way.

The Eightfold Path consists of the following (Table 3.4):

Table 3.4 The Eightfold Path

Right Views	Means to keep ourselves free from prejudice, superstition, and delusion and to see how real life is entwined with suffering.
Right Thoughts	Means to turn away from the hypocrisies of this world and to direct our minds toward truth and positive attitudes and action
Right Speech	Means to refrain from pointless and harmful talk … to speak kindly and courteously to all.
Right Conduct	Means to see that our deeds are peaceable, benevolent, compassionate and pure … and to live the teachings daily.
Right Livelihood	Means to earn our living in such a way as to entail no evil consequences. To seek that employment to which we can give our complete enthusiasm and devotion.
Right Effort	Means to direct our efforts continually and overcoming of ignorance and craving desires.
Right Mindfulness	Means to cherish good and pure thoughts, for all that we say and do arises from our thoughts.
Right Meditation (or concentration) (effort, mindfulness and concentration lead to meditation)	Means to concentrate on the Oneness of all life and the Buddhahood that exists in all things.

Note: The reader may find it helpful to substitute "harmonious" or "appropriate" for the word "right" used above. This version of the Eightfold Path was adapted from *The Buddhist Temple of Chicago Service Book,* 40th Anniversary Edition, 1984.

Buddhism offers that humans are responsible for resolving the problem of suffering, not God (Malothu, 2020; Buswell, 2019). And, by studying and practicing the Eightfold Path, a right view and thoughts lead to wisdom; right speech and livelihood lead to ethical conduct; and right effort, concentration and mindfulness lead to mental discipline. Hence ethical conduct, mental discipline, and wisdom are the three foundational elements of Buddhism (Rahula, n.d.). Through the middle way of the Eightfold Path, with great faith, great doubt, and great determination, one resolves suffering and achieves the realization of enlightenment (Loori, 2002).

In summary, the religious wisdom traditions teach that suffering is a place of spiritual promise and healing, if we would "take up our cross" with conscious intent (Brussat & Brussat, 1996). Finding meaning with conscious intent enables voice, which a caring and compassionate other can listen to and help heal. The possibilities for human wholeness can be discovered through suffering when we engage in dialogue with a responsible and caring other who can touch our deepest sources of existence (Goldberg, 2001). If a person is open to finding and accepting meaning in their suffering, this opens a realm beyond the rawness of the physical or emotional pain they feel. Religion and faith traditions offer a welcoming community to begin one's search.

Social Sciences

Suffering as viewed through the lens of a social scientist takes place within a cultural struggle to constitute our lives with positive meaning (Wilkinson, 2005). We intimate this in the opening lines of the chapter. The task in this realm consists less in the hermeneutics of our mental, physical, or spiritual state, as is the case with medicine, psychology, and religion, but rather in the analysis of social conditions on which suffering depends and, in the organizations that guarantee its elimination as much as possible (Breton, 1979). It is the individual, as well as a suffering public, who demands that those who govern and lead pay attention and protect by creating and providing social conditions that are constructive, effective, and sustainable.

Staub and Vollhardt (2008) recognized that suffering, although a natural condition of being alive, in some if not many instances, is caused by intentional human acts. People are assaulted, raped, and legislated against. Some children are abused in their families, whether through physical, emotional, or sexual neglect. Identity groups are victimized as they are often the targets of harassment, discrimination, and violence, including in the extreme, genocide. In this regard, Amato (1994) noted that a democracy envisages the citizen as having a claim against the whole, and the whole as having a claim against the citizen. Thus, democracy is a community of distributed suffering. "The domestic politics of a democracy will turn in large measure on the issue of who suffers what and why" (1994, p. 26). In this light, Bourdieu (1993) argued that social scientists commit to identifying and responding to the economic, social, and political factors that lead to attacks on individuals' freedom and legitimate aspirations to happiness and self-realization which are determined by manipulations of and mechanisms in the social, public sphere:

> One has to acknowledge the effect it can have in allowing those who suffer to find out that their suffering can be imputed to social causes and thus to feel exonerated; and in making generally known the social origin, collectively hidden, of unhappiness in all its forms, including the most intimate, the most secret.
>
> (p. 629)

Staub and Vollhardt (2008) concluded that our human condition is shaped by our responses to the forms of resistance we face in our local and worldly pursuits of happiness: responses of grief, rage, fear, anger, humiliation. In these struggles and hardships, though, perhaps there is a choice between dignity and despair, to transcendent responses such as fortitude, humor, vigilance, grace, and irony that can simply help lighten, and in certain instances, undo.

There is a great deal that can be said regarding the focus of suffering across the social sciences. This is especially the case with respect to matters of oppression (Steketee et al., 2021), marginalization (Zion, 2020), the effects of dramatic social stratification (Connelly et al., 2021), and the realities of poverty (Lee & Zhang, 2021). As this body of work is both extensive and technical, we would stray too far afield by seeking to address the literature in any comprehensive way.

Education

Perhaps, the conversation of suffering in schools begins with Rousseau's *Emile* where suffering, the detriment of and its usefulness in life and learning, is discussed throughout the work:

> If you let children suffer you risk their health and life; you make them miserable now; if you take too much pains to spare them every kind of uneasiness you are laying up much misery for them in the future; you are making them delicate and over-sensitive; you are taking them out of their place among men, a place to which they must sooner or later return, in spite of all your pains. You will say I am falling into the same mistake as those bad fathers whom I blamed for sacrificing the present happiness of their children to a future which may never be theirs.
>
> (Rousseau, 1762/2011, p. 169)

Mintz (2012) and Jonas (2010) addressed the important distinction in Rousseau's work regarding hardship in learning and observe how Western cultures stalwartly maintain the belief that students will learn best if they have positive experiences in the classroom rather than if they face painful challenges. Jonas noted that "the goal is not to see the end of suffering in schools, but to see the increase of self-mastery, which necessarily includes hardship and difficulty" (2010, p. 52). Mintz (2012) identified two types of suffering in school settings: useful or beneficial suffering and dangerous suffering. Useful suffering is suffering that is inherent to education and encountered by a personal exploration that involves learning by confronting oneself with what one has not yet learned. Students learn appreciation for and tolerance of the limits and vicissitudes of human existence by suffering beneficially in schools. This useful or beneficial suffering in school is characterized by introducing students to the concept of recognizing their discomforts and identifying how they can deal with them constructively. Useful suffering also enables students to understand the suffering of others and motivates them to act to alleviate that suffering. Meanwhile, unnecessary, dangerous suffering refers to child abuse, arbitrary punishment, and coercion; neither facilitating learning nor cultivating just social relations. The resolution offered is in the careful practice of distinguishing between the valuable and the harmful effects of proposed educational experiences.

The presupposition of the existence of suffering in schools is evident due to the commonplace nature of violence and carnage in school settings around the world (Stevenson, 2002; Currie, 2020; McMahon et al., 2020). Harber (2004) observed that schools as a social, historical, and political system are found wanting in that "the sad truth is that formal, mass education schooling—cannot automatically be linked with enlightenment, progress, and liberty and indeed too often can be linked to pain and suffering" (p. 1). He identified the authoritarian nature of schooling as the reason students have little choice in to how, what, when, and, where it is that they learn. Viciousness in schools including the various forms of bullying, from racial prejudice to outright assault and murder perpetrated by students on their peers and teachers, create norms that enact overall troublesome, security-oriented school regimes.

With school shootings prevalent in the United States, as in Uvalde, Sandy Hook and Columbine, the prevalent remedy used by cautious administrators has become a control and surveillance method by the school in the monitoring of students. And, along with the devastation of murderous violence in schools, social-emotional viciousness has grown and continues to be a pervasive and profoundly toxic phenomenon among children in PK–12 schools worldwide (Cohen, 2021). Another instance of schooling as violence is the legality and persistence of corporal punishment in countries around the world and the long-term negative effects it has on children despite empirical evidence that shows the positive effects of corporal punishment being outlawed (Maiti, 2021; Obadire & Sinthumule, 2021). The long-term impact on the schooling ecosystem because of such physical, social, and emotional realities cannot be more disturbing nor be simply ignored. Harber (2004) suggested that global initiatives such as international relief agencies, national and state systemic reform measures, humanistic teacher education programming, and the democratic resolution of conflict are all part of a remedy for reducing violence and its short- and long-term effects on students.

Gaspard et al. (2012) argued a close connection between the organization of working life—whether as school student or later in life as an employee—and the psychological health and social well-being of individuals in their families and community lives. They put forward that the schooling system creates conditions in which those who are not successful beneficiaries of the system suffer psychologically and socially for the rest of their lives without substantial access to a meaningful and effective public arena of debate, decision-making, and action where their voices can be heard and acted upon. They recommended that instead of reforming lifelong schooling, a curriculum should be established that seeks to emancipate people.

Davies's (2012) work on suffering informs school situations as well. Schools often have difficulty accommodating the idiosyncrasies of individual precocity or talent because they must teach a set curriculum and judge the students according to firm standards. Hence, a student's struggle within or failure at school may be due to a number of reasons, including overly strict grading regimes, lack of insight into the creative temperament, strict compliance to external regulations, or perhaps simply a bad teacher. It is also true that educating children who do not fit within defined norms of acceptable behavior or thought can result in subtle or crude disciplinary measures, causing them to be penalized for what is considered their abnormality. Furthermore, children suffer when they blame themselves for their oddities, absolving the school environment of any wrongdoing and enhancing the feeling that it is themselves who are misfits and abnormal. Many students suffer because their budding talents are not appropriately accommodated or recognized in their school environment. What often happens is that suffering arises in the space between a student's tendency to conform to school norms and their desire to develop and express their unique creative, emotional, and intellectual potentialities. Ultimately, students will suffer even as they fight against difficult, mind-numbing routines that keep them from thriving.

Olson (2009) identified wounds inflicted on students by schools. A school wound is a potential reason for a loss of interest in the pleasures of learning. She identified seven wounds of creativity, compliance, rebelliousness, numbness, underestimation, perfectionism, and the average that harm students. A school wound produces students who feel shamed by negative school experiences, or they may believe they are not smart or competent and lack the ability to be creative. A student may be attached to the idea they must have the correct answer and are wounded because of this and may even hold an oppositional attitude toward school, teachers, or other objects of authority. Schools cause wounding through the maintenance of learning environments that are intolerant of cognitive, emotional, or identity differences, and provoke feelings of disapproval of self and shame associated with being distinctive. The pressure to comply, with unsuccessful (or too successful) adaptations to the educational environment, is problematic resulting in a fracture of experiential, social, and pleasurable aspects of teaching and learning.

Meier's (2021) existential framework is helpful for the discussion of youth suffering in relation to schools. While an increasing number of apparently ordinary young people seek out and receive help, their problems are increasingly explored from a professionalized and pathological perspective. Oftentimes (but not always), young people's emotional distress is well grounded in existential issues and the challenges they encounter such as freedom, love, choice, competition, friendship, responsibility, and guilt that are intrinsic to human existence. In other words, students' experiences are directly related to fundamental conditions of existence from which suffering unavoidably arises. Because of this, it is relevant to comprehend the actual lifeworld, relationships, and contextual meaning of another person's life to understand their suffering. So, a critical paradox can exist in response to suffering when an industry may be inclined to pathologize students rather than holistically support them through a range of life challenges. Rather than a pathologized solution, an existential perspective renders suffering as an unavoidable, critical, and even educative condition. To develop an insightful understanding of suffering in schools, we need diverse accounts and discourses that allow us to criticize socially induced suffering, treat pathological suffering, and encompass the suffering connected to existential conditions.

Conclusion

Due to a general dismissal of pressing cultural and climate issues that characterize how schooling is done, latent pathologizing and consequent anaesthetizing of suffering in schools are in turn bringing their own side effects (Davies, 2012). Person to person, one to the other, if we want to know the meaning, moral value, and response to suffering, we have to ask the person at the center of the issue, the one who is suffering (Fitzpatrick et al., 2016).

Let us be completely clear in concluding, just as Driver (2007) noted in her discussion of adult suffering in the workplace, our exploration of student suffering in schools may suggest that suffering is good and that schools are free to inflict suffering, and even motivate students to find meaning in it. The intent of this chapter, and book in its entirety, could not be further misconstrued. Our purpose is to lay out a broad understanding of the nature and effects of suffering in general terms as informed by a rich and complicated body of literature. This background is to assist a range of school workers, and those who lead schools in particular, with insights into the possible dimensions of and responses to student suffering, either as a result of our modern schooling process per se, or as a result of myriad challenges presented within a complex multilayered contemporary ecology of development (Bronfenbrenner, 1992).

References

Aftab, A. & Nielsen, K. (2021). From Engel to enactivism: contextualizing the biopsychosocial model. *European Journal of Analytic Philosophy, 17*(2), 5–22. https://doi.org/10.31820/ejap.17.2.3

Amato, J. (1994). Politics of suffering *International Social Science Review, 69*(1/2), 23–30.

Austin, J. (1999). *Zen and the brain: toward an understanding of meditation and consciousness.* MIT Press.

Benbassa, E. (2010). *Suffering as identity: the Jewish paradigm.* Verso.

Bendapudi, N.M., Berry, L., Frey, K., Parish, J., Rayburn, W. (2006). Patients' Perspectives on Ideal Physician Behaviors, *Mayo Clinic Proceedings, 81*(3) 338–344, https://doi.org/10.4065/81.3.338.

Bemme, D., & Kirmayer, L.J. (2020). Global mental health: interdisciplinary challenges for a field in motion. *Transcultural Psychiatry, 57*(1), 3–18. https://doi.org/10.1177/1363461519898035

Bourdieu, P., et al. (1993). *The weight of the world: Social suffering in contemporary society.* Stanford University Press.

Boyle, P. (2003). The theology of suffering. *Linacre Quarterly, 70*(2), 96–109. doi.org/10.1080/20508549.2003.11877667

Breton, S. (1979). Human suffering and transcendence. In F. Dougherty (Ed.), *The meaning of human suffering* (pp. 55–94). Human Sciences Press.

Bronfenbrenner, U. (1992). Ecological systems theory. In R. Vasta (Ed.), *Annals of child development. Six theories of child development: revised formulations and current issues* (pp. 187–249). Jessica Kingsley.

Brussat, F., & Brussat, M.A. (1996). *Spiritual literacy: reading the sacred in everyday life.* Kayleighbug Books.

Buswell, R.E., Jr. (2019). The origins of good and evil and the challenge of theodicy in the Buddhist tradition. *Acta Koreana 22*(2), 215–229.

Campbell, J. (1988) Joseph Campbell and the Power of Myth -Episode 5 Love and the Goddess Interview with Bill Moyers found at: https://billmoyers.com/content/ep-5-joseph-campbell-and-the-power-of-myth-love-and-the-goddess-audio/

Cantor, D. (2000). *The diseased body.* Taylor Francis.

Carmy, R.S. (n.d.). Kol dodi dofek: a primer. Commemorating the 25th Yahrtzeit of Rabbi Joseph B. Soloveitchik zt"l The Rav on Religious Zionism.

Cassell, E.J. (1999). Diagnosing suffering: a perspective. *Annals of Internal Medicine, 131*(7) 531–534.

Cassell, E.J. (2004). *The nature of suffering and the goals of medicine* (2nd ed.). Oxford University Press.

Cassidy, L. (2010). Picturing suffering: the moral dilemmas in gazing at photographs of human anguish. *Horizons 37*(2) 195–223

Castelo, D. (2012). *Theological Theodicy.* Cascade Books.

Chapman, C.R. & Gavrin, J. (1993). Suffering and its relationship to pain. *Journal of Palliative Care. 9*(2), 5–13

Charon R. (2017). To see the suffering. *Academic Medicine: Journal of the Association of American Medical Colleges, 92*(12), 1668–1670. https://doi.org/10.1097/ACM.0000000000001989

Cho, C., Deol, H. K., & Martin, L. J. (2021). Bridging the translational divide in pain research: Biological, psychological and social considerations. *Frontiers in pharmacology, 12*, 603186. https://doi.org/10.3389/fphar.2021.603186

Citra, R., Syakurah, R., & Roflin, E. (2021). Determinants of medical students' empathy during clinical rotation. *International Journal of Public Health Science. 10*(3), 629–637. https://doi.org/10.11591/ijphs.v10i3.20747

Cockerham, W.C. (2021). *The social causes of health and disease.* Polity.

Cohen, J. (2021). School safety and school violence: trends. *International Journal of Applied Psychoanalytic Studies. 18*(3), 246–251. https://doi.org/10.1002/aps.1728

Confoy, M. (2000) Women and the meaning of suffering. *Pacifica 13*

Connelly, R., Gayle, V., & Playford, C. (2021). Social class inequalities in educational attainment: measuring social class using capitals, assets and resources, *Contemporary Social Science, 16*(3), 280–293. https://doi.org/10.1080/21582041.2020.1805506

Corradi-Fiumara, G. (2015). *Psychic suffering: from pain to growth.* Karnac Books.

Currie, E. (2020). *A peculiar indifference: the neglected toll of violence on black America.* Henry Holt.

Davies, J. (2012) *The importance of suffering: the value and meaning of emotional discontent.* Routledge.

Dein S, Swinton, J, Abbas, S.Q. (2013). Theodicy and end-of-life care. *J Soc Work End Life Palliat Care. 9*(2–3):191–208. https://doi.org/10.1080/15524256.2013.794056

Double, D. (2021). Towards a more relational psychiatry: A critical reflection. *BJPsych Advances,* 1–9. https://doi.org/10.1192/bja.2021.38

Driver, M. (2007), "Meaning and suffering in organizations", *Journal of Organizational Change Management, 20*(5), 611–632. https://doi.org/10.1108/09534810710779063

Ekstrom, L. (2021). *God, suffering and the value of free will.* Oxford University Press.

Elias, J.L. (1990). Teaching as cure and care: A therapeutic metaphor. *Religious Education, 85*(3), 436–444, DOI: 10.1080/0034408900850310.

Engel, G. (1977). The need for a new medical model: a challenge for biomedicine. *Science, 196,* 129–136.

Engebretsen, KM. (2018). Suffering without a medical diagnosis. A critical view on the biomedical attitudes towards persons suffering from burnout and the implications for medical care. *J Eval Clin Pract*, 24, 1150– 1157. https://doi.org/10.1111/jep.12986

Etienne, P.D. (1995). The Christian meaning of suffering as found in the writings of St. Catherine of Siena. Pontificia Untversitas Gregoriana Istituto Di Spiritualita. Rome.

Farre, A., & Rapley, T. (2017). The new old (and old new) medical model: four decades navigating the biomedical and psychosocial understandings of health and illness. *Healthcare (Basel)* 5(4):88. Published online 2017 Nov 18. https://doi.org/10.3390/healthcare5040088

Fitzpatrick, S., Kerrige, I., Jordens, C., Zoloth, L., Tollefsen, C., Tsomo, K., ... (2016). Religious perspectives on human suffering: implications for medicine and bioethics. *Journal of Religious Health*, 55, 159–173.

Fowers, B., Richardson, F., Slife, B. (2017). *Frailty, suffering and vice: flourishing in the face of human limitations.* The American Psychological Association.

Frank, A.W. (2019). Suffering, medicine, and what is pointless. *Perspectives in Biology and Medicine* 62(2), 352–365. https://doi.org/10.1353/pbm.2019.0019.

Freud, S. (1930). *Civilization and its discontents.* Hogarth.

Gaspard, J.L. Schostak, J. & Schostak J. (2012). Suffering and the work of emancipation through education. *Power and Education*, 4(2), 289–300

Gibson, J. (2017). A Relational Approach to Suffering: A Reappraisal of Suffering in the Helping Relationship. *Journal of Humanistic Psychology*, 57(3), 281–300. https://doi.org/10.1177/0022167815613203

Gleave, R. (2005). Sorrow, suffering and evil—Is there reason to hope? Implications for applied psychology. In Jackson, A. P., Fischer, L., Dant, D. R. (Eds.), *Turning Freud upside down* (pp. 80–96). Provo, UT: Brigham Young University Press.

Glucksman, M.L. (2020). The therapeutic relationship reexamined: Clinical and neuro-biological aspects of empathic attunement. *Psychodynamic Psychiatry*, 48(4), 392–406

Goldberg, C. (2001). Concerning madness and human suffering. *Pastoral Psychology*, 50(10) 13–23.

Hahn, T.N. (2014). No mud, no lotus: the art of transforming suffering. Parallax Press.

Hantzopolous, M. (2016). *Restoring dignity in public schools.* Teachers College Press.

Harber, C. (2004). *Schooling as violence: how schools harm pupils and societies.* Routledge.

Hauerwas, S. (2001). *The Hauerwas reader.* (Berkman, J., Cartwright, M., Eds.). Duke University Press. https://doi.org/10.1515/9780822380368

Nunziante, F., Tanzi, S., Alquati, S. et al. (2021). Providing dignity therapy to patients with advanced cancer: a feasibility study within the setting of a hospital palliative care unit. *BMC Palliat Care* 20(129). https://doi.org/10.1186/s12904-021-00821-3

James, W. (1902/2012). Bradley, Matthew (ed.). *The varieties of religious experience.* Oxford University

John Paul II. (1984). *Apostolic letter on the Christian meaning of human suffering: Salvifici Doloris.* Boston: St. Paul Editions

Johnston, N.E. (2013). Strengthening a praxis of suffering: teaching-learning practices. Nursing Science Quarterly 26(3) 230–235

Jonas, M.E. (2010), When teachers must let education hurt: Rousseau and Nietzsche on compassion and the educational value of suffering. *Journal of Philosophy of Education*, 44, 45–60. https://doi.org/10.1111/j.1467-9752.2010.00740.x

Lee, K., Zhang, L. (2021). Cumulative effects of poverty on children's social-emotional development: absolute poverty and relative poverty. *Community Mental Health Journal.* https://doi.org/10.1007/s10597-021-00901-x

Levinas, E. (1999). Useless suffering. Bernasconi and Wood (eds.) *The provocation of Levinas: rethinking the other* (156–167). Routledge

Loori, J. (2002). *The eight gates of zen: A program of zen training.* Shambhala.

Louis, K.S., Murphy, J., Smylie, M. (2016). Caring leadership in schools: findings from exploratory analysis. *Educational Administration Quarterly, 52*(2) 310–348.

Maiti, A. (2021). Effect of corporal punishment on young children's educational outcomes. *Education Economics 29*(4), 411–423. https://doi.org/10.1080/09645292.2021.1901073

Malothu, M. (2020). Buddhism philosophy in India and reality in practice-an assessment. *Journal of Resource Management and Technology, 11*(4), 438–443.

Matthews, W. (2012). *World religions.* Wadsworth.

McMahon, SD, Peist, E, Davis, JO, et al. (2020). Addressing violence against teachers: A social-ecological analysis of teachers' perspectives. *Psychology in the Schools, 57*(7), 1040–1056. https://doi.org/10.1002/pits.22382

Meier, J. (2021). Necessary suffering? Investigating existential suffering in youth everyday experiences of bad conscience. *Qualitative Studies, 6*(1), 116–141.

Mintz, A. (2012). The happy and suffering student? Rousseau Emile and the path not taken in progressive educational thought. *Educational Theory, 62*(3), 249–265.

Morita, T., Tsunoda, J., Inoue, S., & Chihara, S. (2000). An exploratory factor analysis of existential suffering in Japanese terminally ill cancer patients. *Psycho-Oncology 9*, 164–168.

Nietzsche, F. (2014). *Beyond good and evil.* Millennium Publications.

Noddings N. (2010). Moral education and caring. *Theory and Research in Education, 8*(2):145–151. doi:https://doi.org/10.1177/1477878510368617

Norris, R.S. (2009). The paradox of healing pain. *Religion, 39*(1), 22–23.

Normore, A. & Jarrett, B. (2021). Restorative approaches to honoring human dignity and transforming urban schools. In Singh, S. & Erbe, N. (Eds.), *Preventing and reducing violence in schools and society* (218–243). IGI Global.

Olson, K. (2009). *Wounded by school: recapturing the joy in learning and standing up to old school culture.* Teachers College Press.

Obadire, O., & Sinthumule, D. (2021). Learner discipline in the post-corporal punishment era: What an experience! *South African Journal of Education, 41*(2).

Pellegrino, E.D. and Gray, R.A. (1994), "Character, virtue, and self-interest in the ethics of the medical profession: Part ii: Toward the restoration of virtue ethics", *Reference Services Review, 22*(2), 41–52. https://doi.org/10.1108/eb049216

Pellegrino, A. (1995). Toward a virtue-based normative ethics for the health professions. *Kennedy Institute of Ethics Journal, 5*(3), 253–277.

Perkins, W. (n.d.). *A golden chain.* Tulip Publishing.

Pew Forum on Religion and Public Life. (2012). *The Global Religious Landscape.* Pew Research Center. https://www.pewforum.org/2012/12/18/global-religious-landscape-exec/

Rahula, W.S. (n.d.) The Buddha's practical instructions to reach the end of suffering. Tricycle. Online. https://tricycle.org/magazine/noble-eightfold-path/

Reich W.T. (1989). Speaking of suffering; a moral account of compassion. *Soundings, 72*(1), 83–108.

Ronay, Z. (2019). Respect for human dignity as a framework and subject of education in the light of present challenges. In Carmo, M. (Ed.) *Education applications and developments IV.* In Science Press.

Rousseau, J. (2011). *Emile.* (B. Foxley, Trans.) [Ebook #5427]. Project Guttenberg. https://www.gutenberg.org/cache/epub/5427/pg5427- (Original work published 1762)

Rouzati, N. (2018). Evil and human suffering in Islamic thought—towards a mystical theodicy. *Religions, 9*(47). doi:https://doi.org/10.3390/rel9020047

Sahlberg, P. (2012). How GERM is infecting schools around the world? [Blog post]. Pashishlberg.com

Schuelke, T., & Rubenstein, J. (2020). Dignity therapy in pediatrics: a case series. *Palliative Medicine Reports, 1*(1), 156–160.

Siddiqui, M. (2021). *Human struggle. Christian and Muslim perspectives.* Cambridge University Press.

Southgate, C. (2018). *Theology in a suffering world.* Cambridge University Press.

Starr, M. (2019). *Wild mercy. Living the fierce and tender wisdom of the women mystics.* Sounds True.

Stiegler, JR, Molde, H, Schanche, E. (2018). Does an emotion-focused two-chair dialogue add to the therapeutic effect of the empathic attunement to affect? *Clinical Psychology & Psychotherapy, 25*, e86– e95. https://doi.org/10.1002/cpp.2144

Steketee, A., Williams, M. T., Valencia, B. T., Printz, D., & Hooper, L. M. (2021). Racial and Language Microaggressions in the School Ecology. *Perspectives on Psychological Science, 16*(5), 1075–1098. https://doi.org/10.1177/1745691621995740

Soelle, D. (1975). *Suffering.* Fortress Press.

Soloveitchik, J.B. (1958). *Keol Dodi Dofek.* Retrieved from [Sefaria]

Sporre, K., 2020, 'Ethics in compulsory education—Human dignity, rights and social justice in five contexts', *HTS Teologiese Studies / Theological Studies 76*(1), a5821. https://doi.org/10.4102/hts.v76i1.5821

Stefkovich, J. & Frick, W. (2021). *Best interests of the student: applying ethical constructs to legal cases in education.* Routledge. https://doi.org/10.4324/9780367816032

Staub, E. and Vollhardt, J. (2008), Altruism born of suffering: The roots of caring and helping after victimization and other trauma. *American Journal of Orthopsychiatry, 78*, 267–280. https://doi.org/10.1037/a0014223

Stevenson, R. (Ed.). (2002) *What will we do? Preparing a school community to cope with crises.* Routledge.

The New Shorter Oxford English Dictionary on Historical Principles (1993). Clarendon Press.

Tilley, T.W. (2000). *The evils of theodicy.* Wipf & Stock.

Van Hooft, S. (1998). The meanings of suffering. *Hastings Center Report, 28*(5), 13–19.

Watson, J. (2005). *Caring science as sacred science.* F.A. Davis Company.

Wahass, S.H. (2005). The role of psychologists in health care delivery. *J Family Community Med. 12*(2):63–70. PMID: 23012077; PMCID: PMC3410123.

Weisz, E. & Zaki, J. (2017). Empathy-building interventions: a review of existing work and suggestions for future directions. In E.M. Seppälä, E. Simon-Thomas, S. Brown, M.C. Worline, C.D. Cameron, and J. R. Doty (Eds.). *The oxford handbook of compassion science* (pp. 205–217). Oxford. https://doi.org/10.1093/oxfordhb/9780190464684.013.16

Wilkinson, I. (2005) *Suffering: a sociological introduction.* Polity.

Younas A. (2020). Relational inquiry approach for developing deeper awareness of patient suffering. *Nursing Ethics, 27*(4):935–945. doi:10.1177/0969733020912523

Younger, J.B. (1995). The alienation of the sufferer. *Advanced Nursing Science, 17*(4):53–72

Zion, S. (2020). Transformative student voice: extending the role of youth in addressing systemic marginalization in U.S. schools. *Multiple Voices for Ethnically Diverse Exceptional Learners, 20*(1), 32–43. https://doi.org/10.5555/2158-396X-20.1.32

4   Study Description

Frank (2001) asked in an inquiry into the health professions, "Can we research suffering?" Our position is that people can suffer throughout their lives because of events, incidents, or experiences they had while in school. These distressing and painful school experiences either shaped a person's life or hindered their development and growth. Creating and opening this epistemic space for dialogue is a prerequisite for developing new perspectives for educators (Corradi-Fiumara 2015). To understand the depth and breadth of students' suffering in school, we carefully listened to those who have had in-school experiences in addition to capturing a range of feedback through survey responses. These approaches allowed participants to tell their stories to us.

Although we set out to study what people suffered most from in school, understanding what suffering does to people can be difficult to research and write about because it is neither morally comforting nor intellectually satisfying (Wilkinson, 2005). In light of Frank's question in respect to our work, we believe "that even in the face of ultimate human failing, we must be responsive to suffering and attuned to joy" (Klay, 2017). Our resolve as researchers is to be compassionate stewards of suffering by providing the opportunity for participants to express their grief, sorrow, and distress over school experiences and offering comfort, consolation, and a pathway to understanding, support, and ultimately healing. We suffered along with our participants over their school hardships and the social and emotional toll the experiences took on them.

When Schohaus (1927) conducted his original study, his intent was to persuade as many people as possible from all ranks, classes, and professions to help investigate and understand what was wrong with schools. It was not intended then, nor is it intended now, to deny that there are good things occurring in schools. The question, "From what did you suffer most in school?" does not arise from unfriendly feelings toward schools or teachers; rather, the question is asked to get to the humanistic center of a student's painful school experiences, identify, and help remedy them.

> Narrative identity attempts to capture the existential experience of an individual in the story of one's life. It embraces the whole of human life without fixing it into a static paradigm. On the contrary, it consents to

DOI: 10.4324/9780429465499-4

mutability in life, or even further, it welcomes challenges and changes as indispensable to live a constructive and creative life with integrity and cohesion of the individual life as a project for which we are solely responsible.

(Wiercinski, 2013, p. 19)

Through an examination of narratives of suffering in schools, this study aims to contribute to a body of knowledge that can ultimately be useful in providing relief to suffering students in school settings, while providing a moral vision that enables teachers, school leaders, and other caring professionals to better understand and alleviate suffering in schools.

Research Questions

Our four research questions aligned with Schohaus's (1927) original study are:

1. From what did students suffer most in school?
2. What are the experiential characteristics and effects of that suffering?
3. How can school suffering accounts be interpreted considering existing literature on the topic?
4. How do the categories of suffering from (Schohaus, 1927) compare with themes of suffering in schools today?

Researcher Ethics

Studying suffering required us to connect with the inquiry on many levels: as researchers, as fellow travelers, and simply as human beings. Although the typical academic lexicon is for "data" being considered "collected", out of honor and respect for those who participated, we consider the interview conversations and surveys as privileged moments, offerings, and gifts given by people who were willingly vulnerable to our inquiry (Bourdieu et al, 1999; Saldaña, 2015). This is especially the case when collecting the stories and feedback of others simply breaks your heart (Rager, 2005).

Methods

By its very nature, qualitative inquiry is a customized, inductive, emergent approach that permits the researcher more personal input during study planning, execution, and report writing (Saldaña, 2015). In this qualitative study, a narrative inquiry approach was used; conversational interviewing and surveying techniques were the primary means used to learn about our participants' lifeworlds and conscious experiences of suffering in school. This approach offered us an avenue for a reflexive praxis-oriented analytical inquiry, analysis, and writing process. We listened openly and carefully in order to report accurately and clearly what participants said, and, most importantly, meant.

The study began with interviews of people known personally because in order to establish trust when discussing troubling and vulnerable life experiences, social proximity and familiarity are two of the conditions for nonviolent communication (Bourdieu, et al. 1999, p. 610). These initial conversations helped to establish a baseline sense of the phenomena under study and clarify an ethos acquiescent to the difficult matters being discussed. These activities provided structure and insight as we created a working protocol for our subsequent interactions. Additional interviews were carried out over time and preceded a survey that was launched to capture a broader representation of views. The protocol for face-to-face interviews and the online survey were created by keeping in mind our desire to improve the circumstances of our participants, the important identity groups they belonged to, and perhaps their general human condition (Kvale, 2007).

Participants were sought through local, regional, and national channels. Personal, social, and professional networks provided the basis for local, regional, and national outreach for locating participants. Participants had the option of being interviewed face-to-face or completing the online survey utilizing the same questions. Data collection from the survey instrument and interviews were collected simultaneously and securely stored. Subsequent formal analysis followed theming procedures similar to Schohaus's (1927) original study, with minor variations as discussed below.

Participant Sampling

A purposeful, criterion-based sampling method was used to select information-rich cases whose involvement would illuminate the questions being studied (Patton, 1990). Purposeful, criterion-based sampling aims to identify cases that are likely to be information-rich to discover opportunities for program or system improvements because they may reveal major system weaknesses (Patton, 1990). The criteria for participation were students or parents of children who experienced incidents of suffering in school. A number of university students participated from three private universities in the northeastern region of the United States. Undergraduate and graduate students were solicited to participate via flyers and through outreach by university professors to their classes in the humanities and social sciences (Figure 4.1).

"From what did you suffer most at school?"

Research project. Written responses. All IRB regualtions followed. Strict confidentiality.

For Information and to participate
contact understandingsuffering@gmail.com

Figure 4.1 Participation flyer/email.

We also reached out to regional religious, community, and other socially oriented local associations for participants via flyers and through contacts with organizational leaders who connected us with potential participants. A classified advertisement was also placed in the January and March 2018 issues of *The New York Review of Books* seeking a national, albeit random and unique, subsample of total participants (Figure 4.2).

A campaign was conducted through Facebook reaching into the social network's links to professional groups and associations, friends, former students, and other connections. We did not reach as wide an audience through print media as hoped. For instance, the *New York Review of Books* advertisement was successful only in that it produced a limited number of survey respondents and one face-to-face interview. Nevertheless, the contribution of the national participants was beneficial for complementing a more regional focus and ascertaining variation in the experiences and stories being told. Otherwise, because of exigencies of time and costs, most study data were derived through university campuses, a social media campaign, and by personal invitation.

Our aim was to attain 78 participants to discuss their experiences of suffering in school and openly render their narratives. The figure is not arbitrary; it is the number of respondents Schohaus (1927) included in the final text of *The Dark Places of Education*. A total of 79 participants ranging in age from 18 to 74 are included in this study. The largest number of participants (42) were between the ages of 18 and 25. Thirty-seven of the participants had some college background, three held associate's degrees, 17 earned bachelor's degrees, and 17 held graduate degrees. Demographically, 64 females and 15 males made up the participants,

Figure 4.2 Participation print advertisement.

with 61 participants identifying as White, seven as African-American, six as Hispanic/Latino, one as East Indian, one as Asian, and three who did not report race. The largest number of participants in the study are White females. Thirty-five participants were interviewed face-to-face, including 30 females and five males; 44 participants participated through the online survey, including 34 females and 10 males.

Engagement with Participants

Once a potential participant responded to us, we followed up by providing more information about the study, including the fact that we were not offering any incentive for participation other than a potential for aiding in the alleviation of suffering in school for others. During the preliminary stages of the research process, interested parties were provided with clear documentation about what exactly to expect once they agreed to take part in the research (Flick, 2007). To illustrate, participants were told they would be asked questions to help us learn about suffering in school settings. We were guided by an abiding orientation toward empathy as characterized in the quote from Corradi-Fiumari (2015):

> From a generally humanistic perspective, questions primarily exist if there is a cognitive/cultural space for them to develop. We cannot simply ask the question, what is psychic suffering? [or, what is suffering in school?] This concern is a worthy focus only if we are, or become interested in the every-day modes of inner pain, which may be evident or inconspicuous. Although our most disparate forms of psychic distress cannot be approached as factual research, once we have captured the intensity of the question, we can further develop our qualities of observation and … interaction. This epistemic space is the prerequisite for new perspectives.
>
> (p. xi)

The following was shared for consideration at the outset of the study prior to agreement to participate:

> Suffering in schools is an affliction of the mind, body, heart or spirit, or some combination of these elements. It means to undergo, experience or endure, or be subjected to something harmful or painful which is inflicted or imposed on one intentionally or unintentionally in a school context.

By providing our working definition of suffering in school, we hoped to offer a space for participants to feel comfortable addressing the evident and inconspicuous parts of their experiences.

Once participants agreed to be part of the study, the option was made available for either being interviewed in a face-to-face setting or by contributing through the online survey. In both scenarios, we first asked for demographic and personal information followed by open-ended questions related to the research.

The Interview Setting

In-person, face-to-face interview conversations lasted generally 30–60 minutes and were conducted on a university campus in a private office specifically prepared and secured for the study, or in an alternate location mutually agreed upon. If the participant agreed, the interview conversations were recorded using a digital voice recorder. General notes were taken unobtrusively during the conduct of the interview and specific notes were written immediately after the conclusion to assist in later analysis.

A conversational protocol was followed when carrying out interviews, and although each encounter was unique, an intentional rhythm or flow was emphasized that aimed to ensure our participants felt safe and comfortable discussing difficult and distressing personal experiences. At the beginning of the interview, before recording, participants were briefed on what was to follow. As with a conversational protocol, open-ended questions were posed to grant the greatest amount of latitude and freedom in both written and verbal responses. Initial questions asked our participants to write and talk about experiences that echoed painfully among the memories of their own or their children's K–12 school days. The questions, "From what did you suffer most in school?" and "Describe your darkest moment in school?" emanate directly from Schohaus's (1927) original study.

At the conclusion of the interview (and survey), an important question was raised: "When you look back on your K–12 education, is there a distinct moment that stands out to you as being particularly memorable that contributed positively to your life today?" Although we do not report on the question directly within this study, we used it in order to counterbalance the weight of the topical discussion on suffering in school. We were looking for moments or experiences that contrasted their suffering which they felt would live fruitfully and creatively in their memories. [These data and their analysis will be reported in a follow-up study.] Following the interviews, participants were asked how they felt about the conversation and if they would like to talk about anything else. Conversations about the experience of suffering in school raised strong emotions and salient recollections. As part of the study design, we asked at the conclusion of each interview if the participant would like to be directed to a counselor and provided information on campus and local counseling services available at their own discretion.

Transcription

A digital audio record was made of each interview. A transcript was then created via audio transcription speech-to-text software that used artificial intelligence, automatic speech recognition, and natural language processing to recognize speech producing a time-coded document. The technology-generated transcript was then verified by listening to the audio recording while editing the transcript for further accuracy. The 35 face-to-face interviews were transcribed verbatim, resulting in approximately 1,000 pages of transcripts. Transcriptions were sent to participants to review for accuracy and clarity before they were considered final. Member checking was used to further honor and respect the willing vulnerability of our participants (Saldaña, 2015). [Some participants expressed that the research experience provided a sense of relief or catharsis.] The researchers gained valuable insights into their own interviewing style by completing the transcriptions themselves. Doing so allowed us to have a better understanding of the interview situation during transcription, and it began the analysis of the meaning of the words used by interviewees (Kvale, 2007).

Survey Data Collection and Management

We used the online cloud-based website Survey Monkey to develop and administer the survey. Online surveys enhance efficiency and effectiveness by including questionnaire preparation, data collection, data archiving, data visualization, and assistance in the ability to work collaboratively (Nayak & Narayan, 2019). Participants spent an average of 34 minutes responding to seven demographic and 14 open-ended questions. The survey was available for 12 months beginning in December of 2017 through December of 2018.

Analysis

Schohaus's (1927) original study used a thematic approach to categorize participant narratives based on the substance of each "report". Chapter 5 presents a similar analysis using the following procedures:

1. pre-categorization coding of each narrative response to the question, "From what did you suffer most in school?"
2. classification of narrative categories under general themes based on coding, interview process notes, and research memos
3. the organization of narrative reports by thematic category in accessible and readable form

By constructing the presentation of findings in Chapter 5, we hope our readers can uncomplicatedly empathize with the "reports" and are prompted to enter an extended conversation about our historically comparative interpretations, broadened awareness of contemporary childhood suffering in relation to schooling, implications for educational improvement in both practice and policy, and the vision necessary for building mindfully robust and responsive schools that create the conditions for all students to holistically thrive.

References

Bourdieu, P. et al. (1999). The weight of the world: social suffering in contemporary society. United Kingdom: Stanford University Press.

Corradi-Fiumari, G. et al. (2015). Psychic suffering: from pain to growth. London: Karnac Books.

Flick, U. (2007). *Designing qualitative research*. Sage.

Frank, A. W. (2001). Can we research suffering? *Qualitative Health Research, 11*(3), 353–362.

Klay, P. (2017). Tales of war and redemption. *The American Scholar*. https://theamerican-scholar.org/tales-of-war-and-redemption/

Kvale, S. (2007). *Doing interviews*. Sage.

Nayak, M. & Narayan, K.A. (2019). Strengths and weakness of online surveys. *IOSR Journal of Humanities and Social Sciences, 24*(5), 31–38.

Patton, M.Q. (1990). *Qualitative evaluation and research methods*. Sage.

Rager, K. (2005). Self-care and the qualitative researcher: When collecting data can break your heart. *Educational Researcher, 34*(4), 23–27.

Saldaña, J. (2015). *Thinking qualitatively: Methods of mind*. Sage.

Schohaus, W. (1927). Schohaus, W. (1927, October) Worunter haben Sie in der schule am moisten gelitten? [From what did you suffer most in school?] *Swiss Mirror/ Schweizer-Spiegel*

Wiercinski, A. (2013). Hermeneutic notion of a human being as an acting and suffering person: thinking with Paul Ricoeur. *Ethics in Progress, 4*(2), 18–33.

Wilkinson, I. (2005). *Suffering: A sociological introduction*. Polity Press.

5 Voices of Lament and Suffering in School

Suffering Now…

Just as Schohaus's 1932 study produced a range of suffering reports from a singular, thoughtfully put question, we set out here to organize the reports acquired from our own research that are derived from the same enduring inquiry: "From what do people suffer most in school?" Participants provided authentic views of contemporary youth realities confronted in school. Through narratives accounts, voices of suffering are highlights of both individual interviews and survey responses (see study methods).

The reports contained in this chapter are the very words of the everyday students who go to school and a few of their parents. For readability, some reports contain minor adjustments in spelling or mechanics, or have been abridged. From the interviews and surveys, we learned that facial expressions, posture, gestures, word choice, speech, and levels of engagement and intensity of our participants revealed their suffering. However, these elements were not assessed or considered apart from the individual experiencing that suffering. Individual reports are organized under broad categories that emerged from the intersection of lived experiences as rendered through reports that illustrate the suffering experienced by being in school. Most accounts can be viewed as overlapping several categories as they "reflect life in its variegated many-sided aspects; life which can never be apportioned into sections, so that nothing remains over" (Schohaus, 2012/1932, p. 123). Each report is one important voice, and each one deserves intense listening, inspection, deep reflection, consideration, and care. Echoing Spinoza (1677), we ask you to strive not to laugh, weep, or hate the human actions and sentiments you read, but to struggle with yourself to understand them.

The Reports

I Affront to Personhood/Injury to Dignity

Female, parent [White]
Age at report: 50
Years of reference: Early 2000's

DOI: 10.4324/9780429465499-5

I think that suffering in school is actually the confinement of and the socialization of a young mind. There are lessons we all have to learn, but I think it has to be done appreciating each individual student.

We all have kids. They don't come with a script and you have to wing it from somewhere. You have to have some faith somewhere that what you think you're doing is going to be right. As a mom, it was just one crisis after the other, for three or four years.

Ashley suffered in school. When she was in sixth grade, I moved her from public school to this private school. It was an extremely creative, highly energetic, incredible drama program, very appreciative small school. Just a great school. It was just wonderful. Kids were having a great time, and then, a born-again Christian through nefarious ties to the head of the school, became very active and started coming down on the kids about what they wore and how they acted. This was not the school that I had put her into. The school I had put her into was to create the energy for the desire for knowledge and to keep it going. Suddenly, it was like, whoa, it had changed, and Ashley reacted to that really badly. I did not react to it very well. My sense was that she needed a lot of intense help and she was not going to get it from either myself or from her dad because we were part of the problem. She needed to get away and went to a bootcamp in California.

Her emotional crisis was coming. Yeah, there were moments I wanted to kill her. I was so pissed at her for being so impossible, and yet she was never really totally impossible with me. We didn't have that mother-daughter thing going on.

The sheer stupidity of school as a place. It leads us into politics these days. The high school's analysis was it couldn't possibly be their problem. It had nothing to do with them. The school puts a frame over all the kids to go in specific directions, like here's the testing we're requiring of them, but all the other things, parents you take care of that. When there is an opportunity for someone to read, analyze, think, use some imagination it's like, okay, you're done with that. I've seen it happen over and over again.

You know, the bottom line as a parent, you do the best you can. You can't get on your own case because the best you could do might have been wrong, but you have to have that sense that you really are trying to do the best you can. My experience with my daughter has fine-honed my ability to call something what it is. I think that raising a child is such an incredible emotional, intellectual [stretch]. Every way it turns you in to an indestructible elastic band. Making decisions and kind of being on my own with the responsibility of my daughter was a heavy load – it was hell, really hell. It reminds me of everything I learned during that period, and I learned a lot, discernment being a major one.

I think that suffering in school is actually the confinement of and the socialization of a young mind. There are lessons we all have to learn, but I think it has to be done appreciating each individual student. And across the board, automated teaching is just going to make drugs and misbehavior even worse. There is such a wealth in a young adolescent's being and such imagination and creativity and angst at the same time. The way we come up to educating them needs to be transformed in order to be able to better help them become. Everybody does something well.

Female, student [White]
Age at report: 34
Years of reference: Early 2000s

It helped me to recognize very quickly that these were not highly competent people. The staff members were not psychologically trained. Teachers were recovering addicts.

My parents separated and then divorced around grade two or three at which point my education became a bone of contention. My parents switched me to a bilingual private school as of 6th grade that ran from 9 a.m. to 5 p.m. every day for sixth through 12th grade and had about 200+ students. By the time I entered that school I was already having social issues and was a pretty pissed-off kid. I mean people frustrated me to the extent that I would actively go to lengths to alienate them. By the time I got to the beginning of high school I was engaging in physical self-harm behaviors in addition to social self-harm behaviors.

One of the problems with the school was that as wonderful as it was in many ways they had no one on staff who was a counselor or anyone like that. Advisory groups were just social or academic issues. There was no one with any actual psychological training. They were fumbling badly on how to deal with me.

I managed by the beginning of my junior year to stop my self-harming behavior, but then later in the year, I was told in a meeting that was called with my father and one of the people who was to lead the French trip, that I was not going to be allowed to go on it. At which point I was just like, "Well, fuck this," and that was the beginning of a deeper moment. I was already alienated, but now I was alienated from everything. They were basically not letting me go on this trip out of something that I had managed to stop doing already for 6 months. And now they were going to deprive me of this. So, not long after, I managed to get myself kicked out, ostensibly it was for sneaking a cigarette on campus.

It was a cumulative moment, and it was terrible. I did not realize a lot of emotional stress from going back and forth between my mom and my dad. I needed some serious help, possibly to go somewhere that I could just calm down. My mom and I went to an emergency center where they have information. We just wanted to get some information on places, it was completely voluntary, but unbeknownst to us, as we were looking at the information, the woman at the center goes to the back room and files paperwork to have me committed as a person at risk of harm to themselves. I was about 17 and spent 3 days in the hospital. That was miserable.

I ended up having to stay there longer, a total of 2 weeks. They sent me to this wilderness thing for kids with issues. I was there longer than normal because one of the reasons kids are sent there was less mental health and more substance abuse. Hard to find drugs in the middle of the wilderness. The doctors in the hospital said my use was more symptomatic, more self-medication, more effect than cause. This gave my parents time to figure out what they were going to do with me.

My parents came up with a couple of options, but they ended up sending me to a place in California. It was a residential program. I wanted to go to a place where I could finish up high school to have a chance to go to college, that was very important. When I went there with my parents to look at it, the people who ran it seemed to really want me to come because I would be one of the only people who was focused on going to college and therefore would set a good example. That was not what I was looking to do.

It was supposed to be "voluntary" for 18 and above and they accept people who are about to turn 18, which I was, and the reason they could say it was "voluntary." But they took away all your ideas, they took away all your access to money, there was no telephone you could use to call other people. You're an 18-year-old and if you desperately want to leave you have no access to anything that would actually allow you to leave. When you're admitted they try to get explicit declarations from the parents that should the child try to leave before they were discharged the parents would not have contact with them or give them any aid. My dad signed on to that, my mom did not, for which I am eternally grateful. My grandmother was the reason it was financially possible. She paid for the gouging.

Part of the reason I went there was that they had an educational program, and I could finish up with a GED. They had an educational counselor so that once I finished the GED, I could go straight into courses at the community college. I used to joke, the place was the benchmark as to how bad things could be and things could only get better from there. It was rife with all sorts of abuses. For example, if your medicine got changed, you got a 3-day grace period to make it to morning meeting. If you were late more than two times in a week, it meant instead of extra sleep on Sunday, you had to get up an hour early to collect trash, or other things, literally digging holes and filling them back in again.

I went at the beginning of April, a couple of weeks before I was 18, and 3 days before the beginning of Passover. I'm Jewish and I was raised Passover-observant. They had a rule of no phone calls to parents during the first month, but Passover started, and I recognized that I was not going to be able to be Passover-observant exactly the same way I was used to. I could do the basic stuff, order a salad without croutons instead of a hamburger. They had so little experience with Jews that almost immediately they thought I had an eating disorder. Rather than call my father, they simply decided that. They moved me to a different apartment complex for students who might be in crisis or have active issues. I was on food watch, and I was not allowed to go to the bathroom for 3 hours after eating.

It helped me to recognize very quickly that these were not highly competent people. The staff members were not psychologically trained. Teachers were recovering addicts. Maybe the reason my issues manifested in self-harm had to do with the fact that I deeply love many of the people who I was very angry at. I was dealing with being incredibly angry at people who I simultaneously love. That is really confusing when you are like 15 years old.

The residential program was an incredibly invasive place. Whenever the staff thought stuff may be going on that they did not know about they would grab everyone, and you had to individually write out lists that included anything you might have done against the rules and anything you knew that had been done against the rules. No one could communicate with anyone during that time. It was a test of cohesiveness and intended to be very divisive. I survived 2 years in a semi-totalitarian, quasi-socialist dictatorship; I can survive anything.

The real turning point wasn't until my freshman year in college. For the first time in my life, somebody said explicitly in a philosophy class: "If you're depressed, it's ok, because things are messed up, depression is sort of a psychological response when you look around the world and that's ok, it just means you are paying attention." That's not a thing psychologists are into. I never really heard that before. Sometimes freedom requires negotiating through non-freedom in order to survive. That really helped, I mean honestly, nothing really helped with what happened at school.

Female, parent [White]
Age at report: 40
Year of reference: 2018

There have been several different situations that for him as a student going through this whole transitioning process and coming out is very difficult and it takes a tremendous amount of courage.

My oldest child is Jess, a senior in high school getting ready to graduate in June. He is transgender. There's definitely been times that have been difficult. There have been times that Jess came home from school very upset, and as a parent it's very hard to see your child go through that. Our natural instinct is to take care of our children and protect them. I wanted to call the school or initiate a conversation and he doesn't want to make waves. It's hard to be silent because nothing will ever change.

When Jess first came out as transgender he was at a public high school. He first came out to his friends—his few closest friends before he told family. We were kind of in the dark for a little while. Then we noticed changes in him but weren't really sure what it was. Between his sophomore and junior year, he ended up switching schools and going to a private Catholic school which seemed to be a good move for a while and he was much happier. Although some of those friends were not supportive and they were very upset when he came out to them.

I think he was experiencing bullying, but he never shared that with me or my husband. We thought he felt overwhelmed. We thought it was a good decision at that time to move him to a smaller private school. It seemed to be fine there for a while until time went by. I think Jess felt more and more the need to come out to everybody and to be his true self—to live and be who he is. And when that happened it was very difficult to stay in a Catholic school that was supportive in certain ways—designating a special restroom for Jess to use, allowing him to be excused from gym so he didn't have to deal with the question of whether to use the girl's locker room or the boys. But it all brought such attention to him.

There were students at the school who were supportive but some gave him a hard time. The jocks in the school, football players, basketball players, would make comments in the hallways or by the lockers and over time that builds up and accumulates and would be very upsetting to Jess. Teachers were all told when Jess was coming to school as Jess, to use male pronouns and the name Jess. They had to manually change it on their class list. Some teachers didn't comply. It made it very difficult when a substitute came in and was unaware of the situation. They would use the female name because the class list roster wasn't updated and it totally called him out in front of the whole class. He didn't know what to say or what to do because he was in class as a male, as Jess, and the substitutes were calling him by a female name. One teacher for whatever reason seemed a non-believer or non-supporter of transgender people and didn't want to change the name.

Another experience was the school issuing an ID card with the wrong former female name on it and the woman in the school office kept trying to give it to him and he didn't want it because it was wrong. She got short with him and was abrupt and the principal ended up calling me. She shouldn't have been pushing it on him so hard and it was just another thing that was calling him out in the school office where other faculty, staff, and students were around. There have been several different situations that for him as a student going through this whole transitioning process and coming out is very difficult and it takes a tremendous amount of courage. And then when you have to deal with people who aren't compassionate or understanding and you're trying to move forward and forge your way through. There were a lot of times that it just made Jess feel bad about himself or that he was embarrassed in front of other people or other students.

Another thing that happened was he had been at the private school for a while and had made friends there. He was invited by a friend to go to their school prom. That became an issue because Jess was no longer a student there and because of his transitioning status. The principal would not allow Jess to attend. He was very, very upset by that.

He had an issue with his Spanish teacher. She made comments to him right out in the open in front of a classroom of students during Spanish class. The conversations were political during class time. She said she wasn't in agreement of the way Jess's choosing to live his life. Many times, she just would keep pressing like she wouldn't let it go.

There's been times when he's been angry about all of it. There are times he has come home crying. So, there's been a lot of different emotions involved. The biggest emotion from the things he's had to work through with all these situations is dealing with various people. It's mostly frustration. I don't think we found anyone that's fully understanding at either school.

Transgender Male, [White]
Age at report: 19
Years of reference 2017–2018

She would humiliate my answer in front of the class even though I did make it very clear that I didn't want to answer, because I knew whatever my answer was, it was just going to be wrong.

I was not a fan of school. It wasn't the education part; I didn't like the environment. I've gone to private school and public as well. I did well in school, but I didn't enjoy it. In public school I had a teacher my senior year and she was very in-your-face conservative. The class was used as a basis for a political debate about who I was. She would ask me questions that she knew what my answer would be. She would humiliate my answer in front of the class even though I did make it very clear that I didn't want to answer because I knew whatever my answer was it was just going to be wrong.

I wanted to drop the class because I signed up for Spanish not political debate class. When I went to administration it was a lot more about defending the teacher than it was about fixing the problem. He said that she would never knowingly hurt my feelings but that was exactly what she was doing. He was obviously very uneducated and continued to ask questions that were completely irrelevant and personal. Even when I told him I wasn't comfortable answering those questions he continued to press and press and made no effort to fix the problem. He just defended her and made it seem as if I was the one being unreasonable.

One of the biggest issues I had in 11th grade was my name was not changed on school records. You have to have the right name on the register. They wouldn't change my name. They wouldn't change it no matter how many times I asked. I was very persistent and go down at least once a week to guidance and every single time she would say it's not my choice. It's administration and they're saying no. But they did end up changing it after they were smacked with a pile of documents about how it was illegal. But they made no effort. I feel like school people see it more as a problem to dwell on. All they would have had to do was change my name on the roster and that would have fixed the whole problem. But they instead just continued to tell me no. Whereas it would have been something very easy for them that would've highly improved my life.

I think one of the biggest issues is that administration thinks it's almost greedy asking for a policy in the first place. The person before me [in public school] had already fought for the bathroom and this and that, so I didn't have to fight for any of those things. But whereas when I went to private school, they made me sign a document before I started the new year, and the document was very degrading. It said the church didn't accept this and that, and I couldn't legally change my name or do anything medically. One of the biggest parts of the document was about how if other kids are mean to me or picked on me, and if I do anything with that, then it was automatically my fault. That was hard.

I was really fortunate to almost be done with school. I only had 2 years left. If I had a lot more school transition would have been a lot harder. I got to medically transition quite quickly. I think I only had to experience that in-between for a little less than a year and the in-between was awful because it's like nobody validates anything. It's like, "Oh well, you don't belong anywhere." It would have been extremely challenging if it had lasted longer. I was doing taekwondo and was in a reading club and had things to occupy my time. This is one of those issues that's controversial but it shows how much schools are so worried about image that they don't care about what's actually going on.

Female, [White]
Age at report: 42
Years of reference: 1990's

Then the students were rewarded because the crueler and harsher you were to other students the more you were rewarded with power.

I went to parochial school when I was young. I switched to the public school which was very difficult for me, and that's when a lot of my problems started with school. I was molested by a family member from the age of 8 until about 12 which I did not tell my parents about. That was a precipitating factor for my anxieties. We didn't have emotional closeness. I wasn't socialized very much as a child, wasn't allowed to have friends over, and I didn't go to friends' houses. Education was important to my family, but as I approached puberty, I really didn't care about school that much. I wasn't really good. I showed up, but starting in sixth grade I was bullied a lot.

I was picked on all the time. I did not fit in. I was different. I had been very accustomed to wearing a uniform. I wanted to wear the same things every day. My habit of being comfortable wearing the same clothes every day is what started me being picked on. That leap from parochial school which is highly structured with a few friends to a very large public school with no friends, more enemies than anything (for no reason), I just took it and was having a lot of social anxiety. I was having panic attacks at school. I didn't have any teachers who I could trust. I didn't have any friends I could go to. Eating in the cafeteria was extremely stressful for me. I would often go to the nurse's office to get out of eating because it was such a socially stressful environment for me. I started to pull inward. I was acting out at home because my grades were sucking, and I was going to school feeling like I was failing everything. I really wasn't good at anything, and I had no real core social skills.

At the beginning of eighth grade my parents pulled me out of public school and put me into a private school. They thought the smaller class size was more appealing and would be a better option. It was a ton of money. It did not help me at all. I didn't do well. There was no structure there whatsoever. So again, I found myself in the same situation socially not being able to make any friends. During that time my parents brought me in for neuro-psych testing. I actually failed them on purpose because I didn't understand. I thought if I passed the test it would mean I had something wrong with me. I had the reverse idea, so I failed them on purpose which didn't do me any good. So, I'm diagnosed with all these things and my parents are recommended very quickly to get me off to a different place. I had to go away to school and they transitioned me.

Up to this point in school there were times my books were knocked out of my hand or my backpack dumped on the floor. Teachers saw. It was never proactive; it was very reactive. The culture was as if it were my assumed responsibility to take action to stop it. I didn't see the educators feel any alliance or allegiance to the students to make sure we were spoken for if they noticed something was happening to us.

My parents were strict, and they were getting angry with me because I wasn't fitting in. It was a growing volcano that eventually created this perfect storm. My parents at the time believed I was ADHD. I had so much social anxiety that it was like excruciating pain to even enter the building. It was not a comfortable environment. I did not have a teacher or a friend or the guidance counselor or even a coach to go to and say, "I'm having trouble." I learned very early on that you do not trust the adults.

One of the lowest moments that I had experienced when everything came crashing down at once was my one simple, silly mistake that I made. The girls at school, they were extremely mean but for some reason they approached me and asked me if I would bring a bottle of Listerine from home for them because they were drinking at school and they wanted me to bring them Listerine. I jumped at the chance because they asked me. I knew they were using me, but I was so excited that they talked to me. So back then Listerine came in a glass bottle and it was yellow. My parents had a big bottle of it, and I put it in my backpack. I brought it to school and during gym class I put my backpack with all the other backpacks. During one of the games my backpack was kicked by accident and the bottle broke in my backpack and all the Listerine started pouring out.

I was immediately brought to the principal's office. They found the Listerine bottle broken. My parents got called into the school. The guidance counselor came in with the principal and they announced to my parents, "Unfortunately your daughter is an alcoholic. She has brought Listerine to school and children who cannot access alcohol are now turning to mouthwash. Your daughter had a full bottle of mouthwash in her book bag that she brought to school that we presumed she was going to drink in school today. So, you need to find her treatment and find treatment soon."

That moment for me—I couldn't even believe what I was even hearing! I knew I hit an all-time low. I've been previously labelled a cutter, I've been bullied, nobody believed me, and now I'm in the principal's office with Listerine. My fate was sealed. I felt hopeless and very powerless as a child.

In the end, my parents had taken the door off my bedroom and took my radio. I was living in a fishbowl. I was not trusted to be alone. And I was definitely rebelling but not in the typical way.

My parents transitioned me, and I had to go away to school. I got there and in the initial two hours I knew there was something incredibly wrong with the place. The residential school was the continued theme of unpredictability. At any moment anything could change, and the rules changed from day to day. I had no autonomy. I had no ability to make my own decisions. They had a very cult-like mentality. I believed they could control my thoughts. We were very disillusioned. We had no access to a radio or clock, time. For a month we were completely cut off from the outside world. We could not communicate with anyone outside in any way. All our letters and monitored calls were redacted. There was no way to communicate that we needed help.

The school used grades as a very strong leverage point, a measuring tool as to how willing we were to work the program. They transposed our academic performance to equal our conforming to their program.

In a normal school a passing grade would be 65; for them it was 95. They radicalized their academic system. It was like home schooling gone wrong. We were taught to the test because they wanted the top scores. Top, top, top and you had to prove it to them by taking four qualifying practice Regents tests and score 95 or above to sit for the actual test. School was very pressured. Memorization was a key component of survival. I really don't have a high school education. They were weeding us out. Maybe only five of us took the Regents but they counted that as a class so they could demonstrate the percentage ratio and boost their marketing and advertising.

We would have to memorize hundreds of words. We had maybe 24 hours to do it and it was intense. That's all you did. And you could be stood up at any time and asked recite line 29 from page 4 and if you couldn't do that you would be punished. It was continual pressure that never alleviated. You were made to perform music, prayers, and memorize parts of an Alcoholics Anonymous book. The goal was to make you memorize material and be able to recall it in an instant. That happened 24 hours a day. You can imagine for a kid; it was constant memorizing so that it pushed out any logical thinking we may have had.

It was the worst. And I retained nothing. I was mentally resistant to them. I knew what was happening was wrong. I dissociated to the point where I started to pretend that I was playing a game. A game I would play to offset the fear of what was next. I understood these were very sick people. I knew I had no one to tell and there was nowhere to go. I decided I was going to just end it. I was 15 to 16. The program used food deprivation a lot. And I was starving. They had me down to about 110 at my lowest point. I was very hungry and urinating blood. I was really sick.

You could lay in your bunk at night and hear the girls' stomachs rumbling. You could hear it. All of us, we were just starving. I had been working in the kitchen a lot and there was a staff cook in his 30s. He would grope me and then started to groom me by offering me food. I didn't care. If it meant you wanted to touch my breasts, fine, give me the food. I would eat the food while he was doing it. The groping became more intense, but I was eating regularly and felt better. I gained a couple pounds over time. I started to worry and get nervous about what could happen next because it was clear to me he was asserting his power and how strong he was. I couldn't tell if he was going to rape me or kill me. I just had a sense of impending doom.

The last time he squeezed me very hard. I broke away thinking it's about to happen. I ran and told a priest who was on staff there. I said, "Look. I'm being touched inappropriately by the cook. He tried it again. I just ran away from him, and I need your help. Can you please call my mom? Can you please call the police?" The priest told me to calm down, he'd handle it, not to be afraid, that he'd help me, and that I should go back to school.

Less than 15 minutes later I was dragged into the office, sat down on a chair, and for hours four staff berated me. What had been translated to them was that I ran to the priest to admit that I was having a sexual relationship with a staff member, that I felt guilty, and that I wanted to confess. The staff members spat on my face. It was very confrontational situation and there was no way I was getting out of that chair. This went on for hours, and if that wasn't enough they made it out to be my fault. They already knew I had been molested as a child. So, they just tied that into this. They told me I was a slut. I got dragged out of the chair and they stood me up in front of a pole in a main area and opened up what was happening to me as a "house topic" for every student. They announced I was a whore and that I'd been having a sexual relationship with the cook. Then the students were rewarded because the crueler and harsher you were to other students the more you were rewarded with power.

The kids were incredibly cruel. It was like a feeding frenzy. I don't know where I went, but I left my body. I was somewhere watching this happen to someone that looked like me. It was like watching a video. I was completely removed from the situation. And then over the next 2 or 3 days, I decided that I needed to die. There was no way out. It was like I had no choice at all. I didn't know how to kill myself. I didn't know what would work. I figured that I would drink a chemical and would go into the walk-in freezer and take off all my clothes. I would either freeze to death or die from poisoning or both. I'm lying there. I'm freezing. I drank vinegar, got frostbite, but I had failed and couldn't tell anybody. I didn't know when I was leaving or if I was ever going to leave.

During the time at the school, I went into autopilot. I was launched out into the world at 18.

II Anxiety, Stress, and Fear

Female, [White]
Age at report: 21
Years of reference: 2010's

I was always just very nervous. I remember always being constantly nervous about being late— I lived far away from my school(s) and I usually would arrive after the bell for homeroom. I was afraid of everyone watching me as I entered the room This was more during middle school and high school. I was also afraid of giving presentations. Speaking in class. Taking exams. I don't think I ever felt calm about school. In my younger years, maybe third through fifth grade, I would find every excuse to skip school or go home early. I just didn't like being at school. I was a very good student, and maintained my high marks all throughout high school. I think I put too much pressure on myself to succeed that I just was a nervous wreck. I was never proud of myself for my good work. I was never satisfied. My mom also put a lot of pressure on me to get good grades. She would also claim that she wasn't strict, but in reality, she was. I felt so much pressure to be perfect, and then I felt crazy for acting this way. I forced myself to take the hardest classes and keep my class rank high. I never had a study period. I spent most of my time in high school being completely miserable. I couldn't wait to graduate. I cut off ties with friends and ruined relationships because of it.

Male, [White]
Age at report: 21
Years of reference: 2010's

My sophomore year of high school was the first time that someone called a bomb threat at my school and like any threat it was taken extremely seriously. It happened around 12 o'clock. Everyone was super scared—the administration, not that they didn't know what to do—'cause they obviously knew what to do, but this was the first time that anything that crazy had happened. You know they loaded us on buses, we weren't allowed to get our stuff, seniors at the time weren't allowed to get their cars. It just, it was you know, mass havoc. Confusion. I mean I was scared just from the sheer fact of life that the school was going to blow up. And then people saw that there was mass havoc and that we got to go home. And so, it started happening a little bit more often than it should have. Bomb threats were called the next within the year. This was I believe in the beginning of the year before winter break, and then after winter break it happened twice, second time—serious mass havoc. We thought it was just the way—we thought they thought that the first time the person just got scared with how structured everything was and they were going to do it again. So, again it happened like roughly around noon, we had to leave all of our stuff to, had to go home, and then it happened again and this time they cleared the school. It happened in the morning, and they cleared the school and we had to go back to class and then it never happened again. [There were a total of five bomb threats]. So I feel like that situation not necessarily [caused] some suffering but desensitized me in my way of how I think. I think possibly I could be not necessarily traumatized by the fact that that happened but just desensitized to trauma now. And I see it in my everyday life that I always know that there's something worse out there. That's pretty much what I'm gonna say. It desensitized me.

Female, [White]
Age at report: 19
Year of reference: 2017

I was very hyper all the time, too … If I said something and didn't think about things when I said it, because of loneliness, then I just got criticized.

School was 50/50 honestly: like and dislike. I have generalized anxiety disorder. Around junior year of high school I started going to therapy. I'm a very outgoing person, a very friendly person, and I had a lot of friends, but at the same time I'd be very on edge all the time with social interactions. It was hard for me in high school. The atmosphere would make me nervous all the time. I was always a little uncomfortable.

I'm on medication for it now. High school is crazy. It's like you're there all day. There are people everywhere all the time. So, it just put me on edge. Probably freshman year in high school was my worst time honestly even though that's supposed to be the fun year because you're meeting new people and stuff. I went to school with a lot of people who I graduated middle school with. And we all started drifting apart from each other, so that was hard. Everyone was in different friend groups. Like my best friend that I went to high school with as a freshman found a bunch of other people that I really didn't like. They were not very nice people so that was a hard time, and I felt very lonely.

I was a pretty awkward person at that time. I was kind of like the butt of the joke or whatever. I was eccentric, I guess. I still am. But obviously when you're younger that's a big deal. You want everyone to like you. I was very jumpy. I was very hyper all the time, too. I spoke what was on my mind a lot and sometimes people would make fun of that. If I said something and didn't think about things when I said it, because of loneliness, then I just got criticized. I'd say something that wouldn't really make sense and then people would make fun of me. There were times in high school I believed I was just not as smart as everyone else and stuff like that.

I loved sports, but it was a big source of insecurity for me. I wasn't hardcore spending all my time trying to excel at it. I wanted to do other things. I mostly just blame myself. I just thought that there was something wrong with me, and I would talk to my mom and that's really it. Schools have made a lot of ground trying to be a comfortable place socially for everyone. But that's not something the school itself can change. They're not going be able to catch everything that's going on between students. I'm thankful I was steered in a good direction by my parents, and I didn't lash out and start hurting other people. I think at times I definitely did it and maybe not like my other peers, but because of all the stuff I was going through I would be very angry and I would take it out on my family because they're the people I couldn't really leave.

I always thought there were way too many rules like at my school. I am not a rules person. I hate it. I always hated that we weren't allowed to express ourselves at all. We all had to be the same and it was annoying to me. I grew up feeling badly about being different from everyone else.

There's another problem I would say with the school system. What everyone knows everyone just crams information and gets it down to a test and then afterwards it's done. I honestly don't even remember much of what I learned from high school because that's all you do. You just cram and then you forget about it. Generally, it's a horrible thing for people to be made fun of and go through hard times.

Female, [White]
Age at report: 21
Year of reference: 2016

Well [in between] my sophomore and my junior year I was diagnosed with an anxiety disorder and depression and I actually missed 6 months of my schooling because I had a fear of going to school. Because I was feeling physical symptoms and I was at school I was very scared. We found out that my serotonin levels weren't right in my head. But there were stressors in school that didn't allow me to feel safe there…I had a teacher who would call me names, she would call me stupid in class. She was a Spanish teacher and I was never good at Spanish and I ended up having to, I couldn't stay in that class. It was, it was horrible. I think it was the fact that the teachers felt like they can do whatever they want sometimes and act however they want with no repercussions. My Spanish teacher would make us feel very little…belittled…like if we didn't do well on the quiz, saying "How could you not know this?" During that time period from I would say it was January where I started to develop my disorder and not show up to school anymore. And that was when I started to really like stop going to school. I couldn't go for reasons I felt like I was scared I would have panic attacks in school. And I felt embarrassed to have panic attacks in school. I didn't feel safe with my panic disorder. Like if I had a panic attack I didn't feel like the teachers would understand or the teachers would be sympathetic, like let me leave the room if I needed to—especially my Spanish teacher.

Female, [White]
Age at report: 19
Year of reference: 2017

At times I would feel like I could not get up in the morning to go to school because I didn't want to deal with the stress of all day and all work and you needed the time for yourself to catch up so sometimes I did take those days for myself. So, I took the time out of for myself to catch up. Then you come back to school and it's like you missed all these notes, missed all these assignments and then it starts all over again. At points I needed that like mental health day for myself because I couldn't get myself out of bed. I just dreaded going to school because I just didn't want to deal with all that amount of work.

Female, [White]
Age at report: 23
Years of reference: 2010's

I suffered most from being the smart kid, I was picked on for being smart and doing the right thing. I was used by others to get help with assignments or to do group projects and I was left to do all the work. I also struggled in high school due to personal issues with my dad's health. It was hard to focus on school and friends when that was happening and there was no one, especially at school, I could turn to. In middle school, one of my closest friends used me for a school project and then humiliated me in front of the entire class. We had just done a big science project together, of which I did most of the work, and a couple of days later in computer class we were to get in pairs to start a new project and before I knew it she chose to work with another student. That was not that upsetting, however later when I asked her why she had left me for someone else she admitted, loudly so others could hear, that she had used me to do the science project because that was hard but this computer project was easy and so she would rather work with someone she actually liked. I was so upset and hurt I fought back tears and eventually ended up in the bathroom crying. Being the naive people-pleaser and not having many other friends I continued to talk to her and be "friends" for many more years until I finally said enough and moved on.

Female
Age at report: 26–34[White]
Year of reference: 2002

Anxiety, though I did not know that it was anxiety at the time. I suffered physically during my fifth-grade year with terrible stomach aches and pains as I was incredibly shy and was nervous to speak aloud in class. This lasted through junior high. Nearing my senior year, I finally felt comfortable in my own skin and had close friends that helped me through my anxiety. I felt so awkward and embarrassed in junior high that I refused to eat lunch in the lunch room and instead hid in the bathroom and ate snack bags of crackers and granola bars. I am sure some people noticed but no one ever confronted me or asked why.

Female [White]
Age at report: 18–25
Year of reference: 2017

I suffered from anxiety and it impacted many aspects of my school days. I often had pain attacks when we would have to give speeches or present in front of the class. In my junior year of high school, I missed a large amount of school due to my anxiety. I recall many days where I would just sit in bed and cry because I didn't want to get up and go. Skipping school become very common for me at my lowest point. It severely affected my education. After so many years of being an honor student I was suddenly getting low grades because of my absences.

Male, [White]
Age at report ?
Year of reference: 2014

Stress from study usually dealing with other peers and their opinions. I try not to become depressed but sometimes I can get stuck in a rut at times.

Female, [White]
Age at report: 18
Year of reference: 2017

My junior year in high school was very stressful. There's so much to do. I didn't really know what I wanted to do, and I didn't know what school I wanted to go to. And I was a mess. I cried a lot. I cried all the time. I felt like there was a lot of pressure around it. There was a lot of thought around it that you didn't really think about. I felt like I needed to make a final decision right then and there. And that was a lot for me. I supported myself. My guidance counselor didn't. A different guidance counselor helped with narrowing things down, but not the one I was assigned to. I always made myself struggle because I always needed to get an A in everything. I just wanted it. I think it was social pressure.

My school was always firing teachers, and there was a lot of back and forth. So, I had an older man for a guidance counselor for my freshman year and he retired. Then I had a girl my sophomore and junior year. And then senior year I got a brand-new guy right out of college. I felt very uncomfortable talking to him, and I didn't think he really knew what he was doing. So, I didn't really want to talk to him. The other guidance counselor who helped me actually went to my high school and graduated 2 years before my oldest brother. She kind of knew me. She was very nice and very calming. She was more helpful with organizing.

Female, [Black]
Age at report: 26
Year of reference: 2017

They weren't inclusive, they were very cliquey, and I didn't fit anywhere and that was my experience throughout all my schooling, period.

When I was in fourth grade I was at school in New York and it doesn't bring back good memories. It was a very strict school discipline-wise. And as a kid I was very rambunctious. It was a small private independent school. Looking back, if I had been assessed, I probably would have been diagnosed with ADHD because I do have it now as an adult.

I was never diagnosed as a kid only as an adult. I was constantly talking out of my seat. I would complete my work and then I would interrupt others and the teachers did not know how to handle that so I was always standing in the corner in time out. There was always a sense that they were angry at me. I was always doing something wrong. I would go home, and it would take me hours to complete my homework. My parents were always frustrated with me. They couldn't figure out how to get me to sit and do my homework. Along with all of that, I was bullied in that school a lot. I was bullied by the kids in my class – the boys and some of the girls – and the teachers were like, "Oh it's OK."

I was very thin. They used to pick on me for that. I can remember they pushed me down, calling me terrible names, and it hurt me all the time. The teachers didn't know much about it. It really wasn't at the top of their list at all. I wasn't taken seriously about being hurt. We didn't talk about bullying or friendship or anything like that. Strictly academic.

I was the only diverse person in my class. And for the first time I noticed race, because I was made aware that I was the young black student in my class. I never apologized for my race or feel bad for being a Black woman. I just thought it was unfortunate they were are all looking at me because I was Black. They weren't inclusive, they were very cliquey, and I didn't fit anywhere and that was my experience throughout all my schooling, period. I talked to a school counselor in high school, but she was on the edge of retirement and that's really all she had in mind. I needed help. It was clear that I needed help —someone to talk to. She left me hanging. She never referred me. So, the system failed me in that sense, big time. The counselor was strictly about scheduling, academics, college, not so much the personal, social aspects that I needed.

III Companionship and Isolation

Female, [White]
Age at report: 20
Year of reference: 2013

In my mind there was no point in me being social with others because I couldn't offer them anything and they couldn't offer me anything.

My sophomore year of high school I had a hard time. Socially. I was never very good at branching out and meeting other people. I needed people to come to me. I was always so into books and learning and reading that I was never like, "Hey let's go out and make friends." So, I only had a couple of friends in elementary school, and I had lost touch with them going into high school. All my friends from my childhood were no longer my friends. I don't have many friends who I'm still close with. My childhood just dropped off the face of the earth. Everybody left all at the same time. That's when I had a hard time just with school and socially and family life and everything in general.

I started going to therapy because I was severely depressed. I guess loss and grief that I was experiencing with everybody that I was originally close to who just disappeared. To me they were all just gone forever out of my life. Throughout the course of therapy, I had been self-harming and making very risky decisions to try to cope with the grief. I didn't want to go to school. I'd sleep all the time so my grades suffered and my friendships that I did have suffered because I wouldn't want to hang out with anybody. I ended up being hospitalized the week of Thanksgiving of my sophomore year for attempting to take my life. I just didn't want to have to deal with the social pressure of having to go back and face people that didn't like me because of things they had heard about me or approaching others because I was afraid they would find out things about me that weren't even true. So, I regressed from everything and sucked myself into this little wormhole of nothing.

I decided that's where I wanted to be because being out in the world with other people never really worked for me. I taught myself to draw and taught myself to paint. I taught myself all kinds of things. But when I went out into the world the things that I could offer to other people weren't really appreciated. In my mind there was no point in me being social with others because I couldn't offer them anything and they couldn't offer me anything. That was probably the biggest point of suffering that I had in my life. There are some things that you can't really put into words. And even if you can it doesn't really help to talk about it if it doesn't get fixed, because just mentioning the suffering you're going through isn't going to make it any better if nothing is being done to try to fix it.

I never really understood my therapist and my psychiatrist and school guidance counselors. They would all kind of try to explain it to me. But the way they explained it didn't really make sense.

They would tell me that I was feeling all of these sad feelings because of grief and loss. But I already have felt those feelings and they just worsened. It was more like it came with no reason and they're trying to explain something that didn't really have an origin in my point of view. It was kind of hard to get an understanding of it because if I couldn't understand it in my view how could anybody else because I'm the one that's living it.

I just went through school figuring that I'm just going to have to deal with it. Even now there's still bits and pieces that I'll think about. It does not come together at once, it's like every now and then I'll get a bit piece here and there and it's like, "Oh, well that would make sense, my social skills are kind of impaired because I'm more concerned about the past than what other people actually have to offer." It's hard enough for kids in high school to get through whatever problems they're dealing with on top of the stress of school—the homework and the tests and all that stuff—[school responses] are more a formality…with reporting. The school needs to be a more open kind of place.

Male, [White]
Age at report: 26
Years of reference: 1990's–2000's

That whole period where you're supposed to be a kid and explore and find out who you are, I was too worried about trying not to be noticed and being somebody else.

To be honest I generally disliked school. I went to kindergarten at the age of 3½ and apparently, I loved school every day until third grade. For whatever reason I never talked about it. After looking back, ever since then, most of high school I did not specifically enjoy.

I'm fairly convinced there was a time in third grade when we were doing a play that I was singing and dancing to one of the songs to myself at recess, kind of playing around, and it was one of the songs that only the girls in the class sang. I remember coming back after recess and everyone was laughing and making fun of me. Ever since then I was kind of the outcast in class. Nobody ever wanted to play with me anymore. No one ever really wanted to do anything. That was the earliest memory I have that's negative for me. The teacher just brushed off and tried to move on and get everybody to focus on work and didn't really address anything. I remember being surprised and hurt. I remember walking home from school with my cousin who was a little bit older. He wasn't very receptive, like just deal with it. And I never told anyone else.

I noticed a significant change in how I approached social situations where I didn't want to be. I didn't want to be the center of attention. I would latch on to another person that was showing kindness or niceness or at least acknowledged me, and I would adapt to their personality. I would essentially become very similar to what their personality was and that changed every couple of years. If they moved on, I would find somebody else and latch onto their personality. That whole period where you're supposed to be a kid and explore and find out who you are, I was too worried about trying not to be noticed and being somebody else.

For one reason or another no one would really want to talk with me or hang out with me. I specifically remember fourth grade birthday [planning]. The teacher said, "Arlo you can have your birthday celebration during recess." I remember being very excited because I wasn't allowed to have like sweets at home. I convinced my parents and I could bring them because we're celebrating. I just wanted to have fun and enjoy it. The teacher said, "OK, well it's Arlo's birthday today, so let's celebrate" and then recess happened and everybody just left. It was just me and the teacher sitting in the classroom. And I felt like I was an outcast [thinking], "Oh well, nobody really does care." It was tough. Throughout school it was just trying not to be noticed, and I did a lot of trying to forget. I became an isolationist. I would go off to and do my own thing. I was happier not around people and learned how to build up a protective barrier.

Female, [White]
Age at report: 19
Year of reference: 2016

I was really offended. I didn't understand why they didn't want to be my friend anymore.
There was a time during my junior year when I was having a lot of problems. My friends needed a co-op school for one of the sports. They formed and were doing that together. So, my friends made other friends over at that school. And then for some reason they kind of just like stopped talking to me. I don't know exactly why but we'd be in school and they'd be making plans together and talking about making plans with the kids from the other school. But I didn't know who those other kids were, and they never talked about including me or introducing me to them. After, we just didn't really talk.

I was friends with two girls who I was extremely close with, but we were also part of like a large friend group. These two girls had stopped talking to me and that really hurt because I was a lot closer with them than I was with my other friends. They could tell [I was hurt] because they knew how close we were. They could tell something was wrong. I couldn't even really explain what was going on because at that time I was just really confused.

And then the last day of school after we had left, they texted me apologizing for it, but I wasn't even aware that they knew that I was upset about it. So, I was hurt that they didn't say anything if they had known that I was upset and alone and felt separated [crying]. I feel because our private school was very small and a lot different than a public school setting, and I had always gone to private school whereas some of my friends had gone to some form of public school, they really missed it. I wasn't sure if maybe they enjoyed hanging out with the kids at the public school more. I don't know.

I had known my friends since seventh grade—throughout middle and high school. We had gotten extremely close. It was very easy, but then it was easy for them to not be as close with me too. This was the second semester of my junior year. It kept me distracted.

I was playing sports, and I had other friends who were on the sports teams. I focused on my schoolwork and tried to get closer with some of my other friends who hadn't been involved in the situation but knew what was going on. They were trying to help me feel better. I think I was just trying to push it aside so I wouldn't have to think about it. I was really offended. I didn't understand why they didn't want to be my friend anymore.

IV Personal, Cultural, and Social Identity

Female, parent [Black]
Age at report: 35–44
Years of reference: 2010's

I believe my children suffered from being male and black in school. My son was told by a substitute teacher that he would never amount to anything. My son began to internalize the idea of him not succeeding in school. This began to show in his behavior and attitudes. I believe I succumbed by operating in ways that ignored my children's suffering. For example, when receiving disciplinary referrals consistently, instead of looking at both sides of the story I could only see what the school was trying to present and not my children. I was enlightened about the school-to-prison pipeline throughout the journey.

Female, [Hispanic]
Age at report: 20
Year of reference: 2018

And it scared me because I saw my grandmother, my mom and then myself working the same line. I can't let that happen.

Well there is no other escape for me. I felt like college was the only way for me. My biggest motivators are my family. My biggest aspiration is I want, I need to help my parents. I need to buy them a house one day so that when they're older they have somewhere to live. They don't have to worry because they worked so hard. I want to be able to give back to them. And not just because I actually worked 9 to 5 jobs with my mom. I worked as a janitor which is the least glamorous job you could be doing when you're 16. I worked as a janitor at the mall and at some shops around like at Marshalls and every-thing. I worked as a janitor. I remember waking up at 5:00 a.m. to go clean up stores, cleaning bathrooms. And I hated it. I could not stand it. But I did it because my mom needed [me]. She couldn't do all the work on her own. And so, I went with her and I just I could not imagine doing that the rest of my life. And I worked with my dad also several times at his job because sometimes he needed help and he's a construction worker. He puts up drywall and he does a lot of things, like puts down tile and I hated it, and he still takes me sometimes when he needs help you know. I'll go help him out at his job. And I can't stand it and like it. If I hate it I don't have to do it every day. You know I would only do it a few days a week. I hated it. I couldn't stand it. I can't imagine doing it the rest of my life. And it's just, it's just not something I could do.

And over the summer after I graduated from high school, I worked at a factory which was one of the most miserable experiences I've ever had. I never hated something so much in my life. You know I'd wake up at 5:00 or 6:00 a.m. to get to the factory and I would get out sometimes at 10:00 or 11:00 at night and my mom told me to do it because she said, "I'm sick of seeing you just laying around at home not doing anything." I had been looking for another job but I was kind of, I was just like, you know, I worked so hard on my college applications. Can I just take some time, "No you can't slack off." So, she told me to come work with her at the factory. So, you know I went and I work there and I worked in a freezer. And I just remember for a while I had to put my chicken nuggets, like chicken bites into the packages. And even wearing like three layers of gloves, like cloth gloves, like three layers of those and then like plastic gloves on top of that, it rubbed my hands raw because like the chicken was frozen and it would dig into your nails. And so, I would walk out and my fingers were raw from picking up chicken for hours on end. And it was like the people there were…they were all also, most of them were immigrants. There was a lot of Dominicans and a lot of Indonesian people. And some of them were nice, some of them were not so nice. And for the most part I just felt like a lot of the people seeing them there they told me like "I've been working here 10 years, 15, I've been working here 20 years" and I just I could not imagine that. I just couldn't like it. It scared me because I would see like three generations of family working on one line and my grandmother was living with us. She came to visit us and she just cannot stay still, she always wants to be doing something, so, she went to work at the factory, too. And it scared me because I saw my grandmother, my mom and then myself working the same line. I can't let that happen. And I saw it with other people there. It was a very shady factory of children working there which, yeah, there was like 13, 14-year-old kids working there. And you know they'd be there with their older siblings and their moms and their grandmas and their dads. And it just hurt me to see that…and I can't…like I told myself I can't do this. I gotta get out of here.

Female
Age at report: 23
Year of reference: 2016

I'm actually like a really sick kid medically and not like mentally or emotionally but I guess like kind of emotionally, but I got help for that. I had a transplant in middle school, but our middle school is the high school so our high school actually starts in eighth grade, and so in eighth and ninth I was really sick. I was on dialysis. It is just hard to compete with kids who are at 100% when you're only going 40. [I had] a kidney transplant. And then I actually I got dialysis and started again the beginning of grad school, too. So, I just had [another] one in September—my second transplant—so technically I have four kidneys because they don't take out your native kidneys unless the cancer is really impacting the kidney. I never had an IEP or a 504, but for some reason like [the school] just kind of pushed me along. And I think a lot of that was the No Child Left Behind kind of thing. I feel I should have been held back because I really can't do math. I can't do trig and calculus and you ask me to do like algebra? Cause that's what I was there for, like trig and calc, algebra and geometry. I've no idea. And so that was kind of the hard part I think, is just academically. I was just either too tired or not there—and then the other half was like the teachers just didn't know. And that's what I mean, like looking back on it that's where I kind of see it. The teachers, like for some reason I don't know why they weren't fired. I don't know why they're still there.

Male, student
Age at report: 18–25
Year of reference: 2013

Fitting in, socially, was rather difficult at times. That's certainly the most prominent form of suffering I can think of, although I would not describe it as suffering. There had always been a challenge between wanting to fit in and wanting to be genuine. I had favored being genuine over popularity, so this caused me to feel deprived at times. At the time it felt like suffering, but now I realize how important those decisions were. The relationships I had formed with my few peers still hold strong today. I appreciate friendship much more now that socialization comes naturally in my life. Striving for perfection in academics was hard at times, but it did not take me long to realize that I was wasting my time with that stuff. Searching for identity, that's another heartbreaker. Not knowing what the future will hold is a pretty scary thing. It is even more terrifying when you're under the impression that your decisions are final and there's no going back on them. It would be useful for kids these days to know that they'll be changing their minds about many things as they grow older, and that is a wonderful freedom to have. It is hard to remember one clear moment. I remember feeling depressed at times in high school, and having thoughts of suicide, but I never acted on them, and those thoughts have long since dissipated. I do regret being offensive toward my mom here and there. I was not always the most respectful child. There were times when I would curse at her for things that now seem so insignificant. This is more of a series of moments, but certainly my darkest times were when I was taking out my anger on my mom. I did not know it at the time, nor did I have the capacity to understand that my actions were foolish and hurtful. Forgiveness is self-actualizing. My "giving in" to the suffering came in the form of suicidal thought. It was comforting at times to imagine all of the pain being lifted away so easily. At the same time, thinking about whether or not I would be missed was comforting, because it made me realize the love with which I was surrounded. My succumbing never manifested itself into action, thankfully.

Female, student
Age at report: 18–25
Years of reference: 2010's

My brother and I were in the same grade, but not twins, and he was on the hockey team at my school, so he was sort of a "jock" and popular. I was on the swim team which was not a respected team or even acknowledged. It was hard for me to walk around not being known, in the shadow of my popular brother. It made me feel unwanted in school and maybe even unseen. My junior year, I was diagnosed with minor depression. My mom came into my room and found me sobbing on my bedroom floor and asked me what was wrong. After many minutes of me not responding because I was crying so much that I couldn't breathe, let alone speak, I told her I didn't want to live anymore. She sounded so scared when she asked me if she needed to bring me to the hospital. I told her I was too scared to actually go through with ending my life, but I didn't want to live the life I had then in that moment. I didn't know why I wanted to die, I just couldn't stand the feeling of not being happy anymore.

Female, student
Age at report: 20
Year of reference: 2016

I was kind of sad because I had detentions and I got detentions because I wasn't able to do my homework. In my school there was a time when you just go out and play. But the other students who don't do their homework have to just sit and work on their homework and have detention. So, I used to get a lot of detentions at that time, but that made me kind of sad because I didn't have any help or support [to complete my homework], cause my parents don't speak English at all. So, they got the first person. I'm the oldest kid in my family so I had to deal with my family back home. You know it's not easy. It's still, it's still, it's still hard because you know all the house stuff like paying bills and all that. I have to take care of it too because if there are any problems I have to speak to people who call my dad [because he] doesn't speak English. My mom does understand it but she doesn't understand it as much as me and my brother, and my brother is younger so it's just you know it's, I'm, I'm older so I have to kind of pay attention to that and help out my parents. That has been for me, it's been really hard because my parents have had problems since we were in India, so it has made me depressed. They still do...I did have a thought that I wanted to die at that point. I did. It was just one time. It was a fierce fight and my parents fight really bad. And it's just I was so overwhelmed like I just don't want to deal with this anymore. It was that point. But now I feel like I can handle it better. Yeah it was back in high school in ninth or 10th grade. I just didn't want to be that responsible at that point. But now I can handle it better and I can deal with them, I guess...

Male, public servant
Age at report: 26–34
Years of reference: 2000's

High school was a time I was learning to come into my own, and that was probably the most difficult time. I almost didn't graduate on time. I was just learning about myself. Loving my skin tone and just accepting the fact that this is who I am was good enough for me. I feel I overcame.

Female, [East Asian]
Age at report: 18
Years of reference: 2005–2010

I tried to Americanize myself, hang out with friends who were not minorities because I felt inferior.

It was hard growing up as a minority, really. I was the only Asian American in my class. There was a point where I tried to abandon my identity. It was the school system. It forced me to abandon my own language. It wasn't until high school that I realized it wasn't right for me to do because it's something that my parents had given to me as an individual, and I should learn to love myself for that.

I was the only Asian minority, and a lot of people were more curious about my background. But they would approach it in a way they believed wouldn't be offending to me. I understand as kids we're naïve and we didn't really know how to approach those sorts of things, but if they could have educated themselves from it, I wouldn't have minded as much.

It helped a lot when I went back to Vietnam for the first time. I went back when I was 7, but by that time I was trying to abandon my identity.

In middle school it hit me the most. I was struck by my difference in terms of race. I was walking home one day, and I usually walk home with a couple of friends, but that time my friends weren't around. So, this gang of boys were following me, and they kept on calling out, "Go back to where you are from." I was from here; I didn't understand. At the time it made me realize I was different, and I wanted to abandon myself. I tried to Americanize myself, hang out with friends who were not minorities because I felt inferior.

I didn't like my identity back then. It's hard. It's constant; it's every day. Even though I was born in America, the school put me in subjects that were easier because they thought because I'm Asian and maybe an immigrant that I would better understand. I felt bad. They would put me in ESL even though I was fluent in English.

V Lateral Violence (Harassment, Discrimination, and Bullying)

Female [Black]
Age at report: 26–34
Years of reference: 2000–2010

It was as if everyone in the room took turns making fun of me and degrading me.

Throughout elementary school and high school I was bullied by different groups of kids. I believe I was bullied because of my eccentric behavior. I was very "silly" and went outside of the norm of the other students. The other students were not very accepting of this. I was often bullied on the school bus and the other kids would throw various objects at me such as plastic bottles or paper balls. Also, throughout high school I was known as the "White" Black girl which offended me greatly. The other students stated they called me this because I was not a "typical Black girl." My darkest moment in school was perhaps when I was in a classroom in the seventh grade during homeroom. I remember the teacher had walked out of the room to talk to another teacher and at first everyone was quiet. There was something playing on the TV maybe music or a music video, I can't quite remember. I had made a comment about this video, and I cannot specifically recall what the comment was. I believe it had to do with me not liking the song that was playing. The moment I made this comment everyone immediately reacted and began to call me stupid and ridiculous for even making the comment. It was as if everyone in the room took turns making fun of me and degrading me. I began to get very upset and left the room. I had thought of very horrible things like taking pills and going to sleep and never waking up. I remember feeling absolutely worthless. When I came back to the room after cooling off no one apologized and they were actually upset that I came back to the room. I wanted to kill myself that day and the only thing that stopped me was my family and the small amount of friends I had.

Female [Black/Hispanic]
Age at report: 20
Years of reference: 2010's

I suffered from bullying, class difficulties, parental expectations. My darkest moment was definitely the bullying. I did not grow up in a safe environment, so going to school and facing the same types of abuse really made things hard to escape. I decided to drink alcohol and isolate myself. I understand more about my mental health. I now know I have a mental illness.

Female [White]
Age at report:22
Years of reference: 2000's

The darkest moment I had was that I was nice to a person who became a stalker. He would drive past my house and scream my name. He would harass me on social media and would make threats. He got his mother involved, who was just as crazy as him. It was a terrifying experience.

Female [White]
Age at report: 35
Years of reference: 1990's

Bullying between grades I don't know that I had any "dark" moments. It was more just trying to make it through the school day without being noticed by my bully.

Female [White]
Age at report: 18–25
Years of reference: 2010's

Getting ridiculed by a group of boys, during my younger years in high school. This was a huge deal then. I've worked through the emotions that were held as baggage after high school. Passivity. I was very passive during the ridiculing and didn't give them any attention so that they would get bored and stop.

Female [South Asian]
Age at report: 18–25 (graduated 2015)
Years of reference: 2010's

Racism and bullying because of my culture and faith. One day in third grade when my family lived in the Bronx I was heading to my mom's car after school and on the way there I got punched in the stomach by a boy. I was crying by the time I got to the car and my mom was furious that she threatened to kill the boy. People had to calm her down and a meeting was set for the next day. The boy's parents never showed and the principal just said that's how boys show they like girls sometimes. Nothing was done to the boy but my class was changed. I moved on and took it as a life lesson so that the next time I was attacked I knew how to retaliate. And that was in middle school when some girl the morning before school tried to fight me. I scratched her face and fought back because after that incident in the Bronx my parents had told me to fight back if I was ever in that situation ever again, so I did. And I got suspended for it.

Female [White]
Age at report: 55–64
Years of reference: Late 1970's–early 1980's

I was not part of the "in crowd" and was compared to my older sisters intellectually. I was the tallest girl in my class, taller than all but one boy. I was teased about my height, acne, and fillings in my teeth. I had a lot of anxiety and my heart would race. I cried and went inward. Once I showed the school nurse where I had burned myself on purpose as I was unable to feel anything.

I grew up in an era that didn't cater to mental health issues, home issues, or even school issues. It was all glossed over as "That's just how it is" and "You'll get over it." I felt as if I had no choice but to suck it up and move forward. I created stories in my head, other lives where I was beautiful, loved, and cared for.

Female, graduate student
Age at report: 35–44
Years of reference: 1990's

Being a person from another country, and a minority, I was bullied by other students and my grade school teachers. I remember not being able to speak English, and I did not have a translator to translate for me. I ended up having an accident on myself. I was afraid about what had happened; and I was embarrassed. Because of my strict parents, and rules in my house; and being a foreigner, I was not allowed to participate in what my parents called "American behaviors" or I would be in trouble.

Female [Asian]
Age at report: 26–34
Years of reference: 2000's

I suffered from classroom bullying. I was in the fourth grade and was repeatedly pushed into desks and chairs by the class bully as the entire class watched. The teacher was out of the classroom. I became very isolated from my peers. I was very depressed most of the school year. I would look for excuses not to go to school. I would fake being sick to be picked up early. I would skip class to go to the library and read. I would not go to the school itself and walk around the neighborhood. There should have been counseling available or conflict resolution. I was an easy target because I was quiet.

Female, student
Age at report: 19
Year of reference: 2017

Hazing from other girls in my class. They would make fun of me behind my back and whisper about me. It was truly awful. I also had to deal with many incompetent teachers who did not know what they were talking about. It is extremely frustrating when you know more about a subject than your supposed "teacher." My darkest moment in school was when I would hide out in the bathroom in between classes just so that I would not have to see other people.

Male, student [Hispanic]
Age at report: 21
Year of reference: 2013

The hierarchy of the school systems in the small places where I went brought me down.
And I did not like that.

I honestly did not like school. In grade school we had a band program and I really appreciated that because I like music. And during those early years everyone kind of did something musical. We were all kind of equal. Then in middle school I really noticed the parting of ways. Some of the students moved on to the athletic teams like basketball. We really separated into cliques and we weren't the people we used to be. I noticed myself being looked down upon. And I didn't like or appreciate that. So, in high school I quit the band because I thought that would better my situation. But it didn't really. The hierarchy of the school systems in the small places where I went brought me down. And I did not like that.

I let my hair out a little bit. It was bushy like an afro, just nuts. So, in sixth grade I was sitting in band. The guys who eventually left the band to join the basketball team sat right behind me in band, and one day I noticed something like a feeling in the back of my head. I wasn't sure what it was. I went back to reach and noticed there were a bunch of little paper balls in my hair. And when they noticed that I noticed they burst out laughing. Apparently during the whole class period, they had been sitting behind me seeing who could get the most balls in my hair. And honestly it was shocking. I knew them, I grew up with them. They were supposedly my friends. And here they are having a joke at my expense. And honestly it was very traumatic. After class I went to the bathroom and tried to recompose myself. I cried a little bit. I was very upset. At that moment I decided I didn't want to be in band anymore. So next year they left band for the basketball team. I left band and looked for other related arts classes.

Other students had noticed what was happening and they were very upset for me. In my next class they all approached me and stuck up for me. One of the supportive guys approached the three basketball guys and told them, "Hey that's not cool, you guys can't do that. That's bullying." And they came up to me and they apologized. At that moment it didn't feel real. It was the norm—people were telling them to apologize so they did it. After that I tried not to associate much with them, but I didn't really confront them. I tried to stay away because I wanted to avoid them as much as possible. It was just one key moment that really changed the course of my life.

During high school I was able to coast. I made honor roll every chance I had. I graduated with a class of about 300 and I was in the top 20, I think. I'm Peruvian, so Hispanic, and I guess the nickname George Lopez was funny because I liked his show. I thought he was a funny guy. But it wasn't until later when I became aware of things like race, racism, and stereotypes that I realized, "Wow that's not cool, that that was offensive." I tried to close myself off somewhat after sixth grade and for the remainder of my middle school years. I retreated into myself and I stopped participating in things and some people didn't notice that. I never got that full experience of participating in things.

Male, photographer [Native American, Honduran]
Age at report: 26–34
Years of reference: 1980–1990's

I hated going home, and I hated going to school. I became very introverted and quiet. I never wanted to be shy or quiet. I really wanted to have a lot of friends and be liked.

From K through seventh grade I was severely bullied. I say severe because there were times I ran home in pain or times I was called racial slurs. My mother was a teacher, and I feel that made most teachers like me. I was often seen as teacher's pet. I was very smart and smart always seemed to translate into weakness by others. Now most bullying is justified by the bully's own insecurities, and I believe that to be true. For a long time, I was made fun of because my mother beat me.

Part of the fourth grade curriculum was focused on the Native American history of New York State. Knowing I was indigenous, a boy called me Squanto and eventually everyone did. I remember telling the teacher and she did nothing. Later in the year I called a Jewish student a Nazi when he was bullying me. He told the teacher, and I was in a lot of trouble. The teacher was also Jewish. Looking back now I realize it was the first time I had ever experienced a type of discrimination. I was the minority in the class, and it didn't matter. My ethnicity was made the subject of ridicule. There was a parent-teacher conference with me in the room. It was made clear to me that I did something wrong. About being called Squanto, I was told it was just boys playing around and poking fun. I cried a lot. I hated going home, and I hated going to school. I became very introverted and quiet. I never wanted to be shy or quiet. I really wanted to have a lot of friends and be liked.

In high school, a former bully ended up becoming a very good friend. He apologized and felt terrible for the way he acted. I spent most of high school struggling with my racial identity. I found it hard navigating a world that said I sounded and acted White when I wasn't. I wasn't Latino enough to be Latino either. I never felt accepted by my peers, so I attempted to "pave my own way." I dressed and acted how I wanted to not have to fit into any one group. I was successful and considered popular in school, but I was unhappy.

Female, therapeutic horse trainer [White]
Age at report: 55–64
Years of reference: 1970's

I was bullied by a girl that lived across the street from me. Her friends would routinely ambush me on the way to and from school and physically assault me. My parents and the school intervened which made this situation worse. This girl and her friends would destroy our property and spread rumors about my family. In seventh grade a girl planned to beat me up after school with a group of onlookers. I had no idea about any of this yet dozens of students did and were present at location behind a factory. I was lured there by someone I thought was a friend and then assaulted while others looked on. An adult witnessed this and then intervened. This was experienced off of school property but was orchestrated by the students during school hours.

Female, student [White]
Age at report: 19
Years of reference: 2010–2015

It was hard to make new friends when starting high school because I did not know anyone prior to starting. I was bullied once in middle school for being quiet.

VI *Educator Indiscretion, Impropriety, and Transgression*

Female [White]
Age at report: 65–74
Years of reference: 1960's

The nuns were very strict. You got one chance and after that you were "bad." I was afraid to make a mistake. I was afraid to ask to go to the bathroom. In eighth grade I saw a nun bloody a boy's nose with a slap across the face and not allow him to go to the lavatory because he didn't know the part of speech of a word in a sentence on the board. That nun was the worst, but there were others who were verbally abusive as well. E.g., one in particular who would say, "People! How base can you be?" if we were just talking before class. In grade school we had arithmetic drills and if a student got an answer wrong, the nun would say something like, "Stand like a moron." I guess there were a lot of dark moments that were infused with shame.

Male, contractor [Hispanic]
Age at report: 55–64
Years of reference: Late 1970's

Mr. B. paddled the student. The classroom was horrified. Several students gasped and I remember a few students started to cry…he would verbally berate students, especially students that would hesitate when they gave an answer in class."
I recount three teachers during the course of my high school education (seventh–12th grades) that stand out with regard to suffering. Each were male and were verbally, physically, and emotionally abusive. The first teacher, Mr. B (names are being altered as I still have lingering effects from the abuse I sustained) was

my seventh grade geography teacher. On the very first day of class, he physically paddled a student that was 30 seconds late for class. The student tried to explain what a reason for their tardiness, Mr. B did not want to hear an excuse. Mr. B. asked the student "Were you late?" The student said "Yes," and so Mr. B. paddled the student. The classroom was horrified. Several students gasped and I remember a few students started to cry. In addition to the physical abuse he perpetrated, he would verbally berate students, especially students that would hesitate when they gave an answer in class. Students were afraid to answer questions that were posed during class. I think halfway through the school year, Mr. B. recognized this hesitation, so he implemented a new tactic. If he asked a question, and no one answered, he threatened to paddle the entire class. When students began to raise their hand, Mr. B. would paddle them for answering incorrectly. Mr. B. paddled female and male students equally. One day towards the end of school year, a female student was being paddled, and a male student spoke up; that male student was paddled and also given 2 weeks of detention for questioning Mr. B's disciplinary decisions. That was my first experience of cruel punishment in school that resulted in emotional suffering. In eighth grade, I had a teacher, Mr. A. that was my history teacher. And although he was not as physically abusive, he was worse, because he would use emotional abuse on his students. He would paddle students for not doing their homework, and on occasion would paddle students for giving incorrect answers to his classroom questions; but was very emotionally abusive. He would talk often about how he could make life very hard for students and would threaten to write notes within our school records that would prevent us from being able to get into colleges, trade schools, or be able to get a job. He would "befriend" certain students and get information from them that he brought up often in class. Mr. A. also would spread misinformation about students with the students that he befriended such as: a certain student was a drug addict, or someone was gay. This emotional abuse had a profound impact on me psychologically, and was instrumental in my development of being a guarded and mistrustful adolescent. The third teacher was my 10th grade civics teacher, Mr. N. He used corporal punishment and would verbally berate his students. He used references about God to justify his use of physical punishment and would use his very conservative values as a means to be "judge, jury, and executioner." If a student misbehaved in any manner, Mr. N. would stop class, give a heated sermon that ended in the physical punishment of the student in front of the class (as was the case for each of the two other teachers).

The darkest moment in school related to a teacher I had for English, Mr. S. After my experiences with the three verbally, physically, and emotionally abusive teachers, I tried to form close positive relationships with my teachers. And although I was very mistrustful and guarded, I tried to portray a closeness to my teachers as a means of defense and protection. And in this spirit, I formed a close relationship with my English teacher in 11th grade. My relationship became very close, with me staying after school on some occasions to assist this teacher with class projects or to help him grade quizzes. On one occasion, Mr. S. invited me to his home to meet his cats and asked if I cared for his cats while he was away one weekend, he would pay me. I declined the offer. Mr. S., from that point on, was very distant and my grades noticeably declined after this refusal. I have a close friend who was a grade younger than me. He states that he experienced a similar situation, and on one visit became very uncomfortable and believes to this day that he was being groomed to be taken advantage of (sexually). I was sexually assaulted when I was 14 years old, and as a result of this assault, learned to be very mindful of my surroundings. I did not get good vibes from this teacher, and to this day, am very suspicious of this teacher's motivations. I believe that I developed, at a young age, trauma responses to situations. I believe that as a result of the abuse that I witnessed in school, that I respond in an involuntary manner when someone raises their voice, when someone uses physical aggression, or when someone is emotionally abusive towards another person.

Female, art therapist [White]
Age at report: 45–54
Years of reference: 1980's

Mean girl type of bullying, I didn't dress cool and I had a lot of body issues that made feeling confident extremely difficult. I was also a slow learner, I had teachers give up on me more than once which made me feel unteachable and stupid, math especially. I was never offered extra help or attention, just hostility. I had an especially cruel, punitive, and abusive teacher in the fifth and sixth grades. She disciplined by humiliation, and I was really afraid of crossing her or getting on her radar at all. Once my grandmother was staying with us while my parents were out of town and I forgot to have her sign my homework. I was terrified of not having what I needed so I forged her name, apparently doing a bad job of it. The teacher caught me, yelled at me and paraded me around to other nearby teachers to spread my shame all over the school. This was an other-level offense because it involved lying, something I was not known to do. I remember feeling that I had no defense, explaining that I was too afraid to not have the stupid signature was not an option, I knew that the teachers and my grandmother and my parents were in agreement with my teacher and there was no one who cared about my side of the story. My teacher wrote a note home, saying I lied and going on and on about this terrible thing and I just had to take the hit. I felt totally isolated and humiliated, and like no one cared that I felt that way. To this day, I harbor a powerful (though irrational) hatred of this teacher who taught me nothing but that if I was going to lie I better not get caught.

Male, architect [White]
Age at report: 45–54
Years of reference 1970-1980's

"I was spanked with a paddle in front of other students for not being able to finish reading Tom Sawyer."
I was raised in a military family, and thus my primary education experiences were inconsistent between first grade and ninth grade. I can remember having

to adjust to not only different teaching styles, teacher temperaments and grading systems, but to also having to spend mental energy adapting to new social situations and physical environments. In addition, in 1975 the state of Alabama allowed corporal punishment by teachers and I was spanked with a paddle in front of other students for not being able to finish reading *Tom Sawyer*. This embarrassment haunted me for and added to my negative appreciation of reading at the time. Our final move was to the suburbs of Washington, DC where my parents soon found that my reading comprehension tested much lower compared to my peers, and as a result I was place in remedial reading during my sophomore year of secondary education. As a teenager who was already self-conscious from physical weakness and scares associated with two open-heart surgeries, having to spend time in a special reading class was difficult and was amplified from the pressure my parents to earn college-worthy grades. This resulted in extreme social discomfort and disassociation with others. Thankfully, my primary reading teacher specialist, Mrs. Grandin, took the time to talk to me about my experiences and patiently helped me to understand the key reasons for my reading deficiencies. To everyone's surprise, including myself and my parents, I later tested at a 99% reading comprehension level compared to other students in the county I was living and I was then placed in advanced English with peers whom I before thought were beyond my stature and I was soon reading and writing a comparison/contrast of the Joseph Conrad's *Heart of Darkness* with the film adaptation of the book by Francis Ford Coppola's *Apocalypse Now* for my semester paper. This recognition changed my appreciation of not only teachers, but it also gave me a new level of self-confidence which suddenly changed the calculus of my life.

However, I had the same issue with math, except there was no math specialist. The first day that I had to attend remedial reading in the classroom adjacent to the standard English classes where all the non-deficient students could see. Math, specifically algebra, was the other insecurity, however I did not feel as alone in that setting as many of my peers seemed just as insecure. However, I remember trying very hard to study for a midterm exam only to be handed the exam back that had a large 29% on it. My heart fell out of me, and I remember our teacher stating that only the students who received 80% or more should consider careers in science, engineering, and even architecture. But she did not mention artist. As I became withdrawn and ashamed that I was not as good as other students my age, I spent all of my time drawing buildings, houses, or cars that did not exist and building increasingly difficult models from kits. Often without the need for the instructions. I remember being happy when my father was deployed and scared when he returned. I remember him throwing away many of my models once saying they were a waste of time and they were why I did not study enough. I keep or photograph all of my study models now.

Female, customer service representative [Hispanic]
Age at report: 18–25 (graduated 2016)

A teacher told a student I was pregnant my senior year and my whole class found out. I wrote an essay about it in my English class but no one knew at that time because it was still the beginning. My English teacher told another English teacher in the room next to hers which wasn't a big deal and then that teacher went and told a student in my grade and it went around the school when I wasn't ready to tell people. I know it was a scary moment that I knew that everyone else knew. It wasn't a good experience. There shouldn't be any gossip going on between a teacher and a student. The teachers should be professional enough to know that that is wrong. I felt that the teacher and my classmates were judging me in a way, and I wanted to prove to them that having a baby isn't going to get in my way.

Male, [White]
Age at report: 20 (graduated 2015)
Years of reference: 2000's

Well for me I was diagnosed with dyslexia when I was like 5 years old. So, with that in mind, dyslexia as it is looked at through the education system, it's merely just a learning disability. So, with that in mind, I took with me for the longest time that I was not good enough or not smart enough and that really reflected on the way I performed in school, as I felt like there's no point or that my effort wasn't good enough. So, it definitely reflected on the quality that I was putting out when I was in high school. They gave me a 504 program so I would be placed in front of the classroom, they would give me shortened lists for spelling tests. They would give me more time [on tests] and for the most part, I didn't actually utilize any of these because even though I did have doubts about my own academic capability. Then I saw that by doing that it wouldn't necessarily solve the problem because that was not challenging me at all. So how does one transcend their disability if they are not challenged?

Female [White]
Age at report: 19
Years of reference: 2010's

When I was still at high school, I suffered from bullying and isolation, even from staff members. In fifth grade, I had a teacher who isolated me from the classroom, even going as far as moving my seat away from my peers. That same teacher also told parents at conferences to keep their child away from me. Another painful time was during sixth grade when I was bullied on a daily basis. Every day I was told that I should kill myself by other students while staff members did nothing about the bullying. In high school, I was threatened to be jumped by a group of boys I did not know, which I reported to my guidance counselor. My guidance counselor told me that my anxiety was "too high" for me to function in a school setting. She also implied that the reason boys were trying to jump was because she believed I dated one of the boys, despite the fact I told her I didn't know them since I was new to the school My darkest moment in school had to be where I felt like an outcast compared to my peers. I felt completely alone, even if I was in a crowded classroom. I, also, felt like I didn't fit in with my peers.

Male [Afro-Trinidadian]
Age at report: 26–34
Years of reference: 1990's

In elementary school I had a teacher who was a germophobe. I did not have the best immune system as a child and when I would get sick she would yell at me and put me in the corner of the room by myself. She would tell the other kids, "Don't talk to him he's gross" and the entire class would say "eww" and ignore me. If I sneezed enough times she'd send me outside the classroom. A teacher with a mental disorder gave me grief as a child. My mom came into the school after this went on long enough and put her in her place.

In either fourth or fifth grade, I would wait for my mother or sister to come pick me up from school at a shoe store that was right up the block. One day two men came into the store with guns and robbed the place. There was a middle-aged Hispanic man wearing sunglasses and a baseball cap who pointed a gun at me—a child. Like I was going to do something to him. That memory stayed with me and bothered me for a long time while I was a kid.

Things were not that great at home. My dad was abusive to my mom and smacked me around. Junior high school was tough for me because I did not know how to handle it. I would get into a lot of fights at school, show up late a lot, and my grades were poor. I walled myself up and would not pay attention to the teachers. When kids would all group up and chat, I was often by myself. Nothing interested me and I disliked everyone.

I was miserable all of the time and kept to myself. I would pick fights with other kids and often get in trouble. I got suspended as well because of my actions. I succumbed to this because it was a lot to deal with in such a bad home environment. Nothing was clear, everything was a fog. I started smoking cigarettes at 13. I used to cut classes to go to play video games back when arcade machines were a thing, or I would just walk around in the park by myself.

Male [White]
Age at report: 35–44
Years of reference: Late 80's – early 90's

When I was in elementary school we had open classrooms. During that time period I had difficulty paying attention and struggled with work. In elementary school I did poorly because I could not pay attention. My teachers did not see my potential as a student and failed to challenge me appropriately. Also, in high school, my school guidance counselor tried to discourage me from taking advanced classes in high school because he did not think I had the potential to do well. When I was in sixth grade I was reprimanded for completing other students' math workbooks. The irony of the situation was that I was placed in the lowest math group for my grade and midway through the year I was so bored in class and completed all of my workbook pages for the year. Since I had nothing to do in class I asked my peers if I could do their work in order to keep myself busy. When I look back on this situation I wish my teacher realized my potential and challenged me. I also realize that I missed out on my elementary years of education because no teacher recognized my potential as a student. When I was in high school I had a guidance counselor tell me that I could not take advanced math classes since my grades were not up to his standards. I saw this as a personal challenge and for the last two semesters I scored perfectly on every test/quiz.

Female, student [White]
Age at report: 19 (graduated 2016)
Years of reference: 2000's

Honestly, I think there are some really, really cruel teachers, and I think they gave points and extra points and stuff to their favorite students. I know in one English class this kid got 80s on all his exams and somehow ended up getting 100 for the quarter. My English teacher wasn't really a fan of me. She just didn't really like me in general. I don't know what it was, but she had something against me. I specifically remember when I needed extra time on a test, and another favorite boy needed extra time too. She made a big to-do out of the extra time, and yet on state standardized tests that we took for her in class she was like, "Oh you guys can take all the time you need…this counts towards the school." She didn't care about personal grades, but she cared about her students' performance on a standardized test.

That really aggravated me because I always work so hard at everything and then to be told, "Oh well too bad, you can't finish the test." That was one particular time that really bothered me the most. There were other times where I've seen teachers give grades to students that didn't earn them. But that situation definitely offended me the most and definitely stuck with me the most.

I was pretty angry. I was frustrated. I cried. In my salutatorian speech I said, "Don't let anybody bring you down." School is not always fair. And it's not always about how hard you work to the best of your ability. Sometimes it's about who you know depending on where you go. That's what I think. College is a new start. I'm on a different level. I'm with different people. The teachers are much different here in my opinion. It makes me want to work harder. I just feel like it's never enough.

VII Corporeal Disaffection—Physicality

Female, parent [White]
Age at report: 50
Years of reference: 2010's

He wasn't in physical pain, it was more an emotional, psychological pain through school.

It was hard with Wes. Middle school was hard. Wes was staying the same size because of his birth defect. He was very competitive in sports and he could see the difference. He wasn't looked at the same way. He was really starting to look different than everybody else because his whole neck was fused. As a mother I dismissed it. He wasn't in physical pain, it was more an emotional, psychological pain through school. He was a high-functioning child with a disability. When he was little, he had to wear a halo. His neck was fragile. When he had his first surgery he was 4 and turning 5. He had the halo for 6 months and the doctor broke the news to us that the bone didn't solidify. Bone liquefies and then it hardens up and the bone that they grafted from his hip to his neck didn't solidify. So, they had to redo the surgery and he was in the halo for at least another 6 months. Wes also has a learning disability.

Kids started being different to him. Everybody was always nice to him at school and they were friends with him but nobody would ask him to go out and do things. And that carried over into high school. Back in seventh grade Wes broke down crying to me. We were talking about sports and all the sudden he started crying, "I just want to be normal. I just want to be normal like everybody else." I'm his mother and I don't want him to know how my heart is broken for him. "If I didn't have this stupid birth defect, I'd be so much better." He didn't come out and say he'd be more liked, but I think he felt like that he'd belong.

We had other times throughout seventh, eighth, ninth, 10th grade where he would get mad at me because parents who were all friends would all get together with kids and Wes got excluded from that. I remember him having a crying fit over that one time and he said, "It's all your fault. If you and Daddy hung out with their parents and went out with them then they would be friends with me. And then they would include me." My husband and I were not materialistic, that's not us. We're happier sitting home on New Year's Eve and falling asleep on the couch than going out and having to put on a big ta-da. But that hurt Wes socially because of us.

When Wes got to high school, he was playing baseball. He was very good. But the baseball coach did not look at Wes as being good. Part of it was political. And a lot was because of his size and that he couldn't turn his neck. But, Wes was better at playing third base than a lot of kids. He could make the throw because he was stronger. And even though he couldn't turn his neck he had always compensated. His father worked with Wes since he was little—helped him to adjust and adapt. The coach didn't look at Wes like that. It was very frustrating for us.

I don't think people were consciously being biased, but I think it's an unconscious thing that they think: "Oh he's smart, he's a nice kid, but he can't turn his head so what's going to happen?" So, powerlifting came in because Wes was trying to overcompensate for his disability. He's always been very driven. He just has that driven personality. This goes way back. We had free weights in our basement. He would come home, eat dinner with us, and then do a separate workout for an hour or two. I think he felt if he could get stronger and faster then he'd be the best baseball player. Sports was a way for him to escape being different because it made him feel more like everybody else. But after he would leave the field or gym kids would just exclude him.

There were different obstacles in high school. It was heartbreaking in high school when Wes wanted to go to homecoming and to the prom. He could never get a date, even with a family friend. Every time he wanted to go to homecoming or prom he got turned down except for senior year. One kid was cruel. Every time he would see Wes he'd say "Oh, here comes the little leprechaun today" with the whole hallway filled. He would say it day after day. Wes pretended he didn't hear it or it didn't bother him, as if he'd just blow it off. But it was hurting him terribly. I finally told the school. A lot went down, and he stopped and apologized.

In the middle of his junior year, Wes worked out in the field house where the powerlifting coach kept saying to him, "You should come out for the team. You could really help us. I know you would do good." Wes explained that his doctors wouldn't let him participate. So, we went to Philadelphia for a checkup. His father told the doctors that the powerlifting coach has been after Wes and he's wondering if you think he could go out for the team. They conferred and said, "You know what Wes, go for it." So, he went for it and that's how it all started. The coach looks at Wes like he doesn't have a birth defect. *He looks at him like we look at him and he doesn't see the birth defect.* He will say to Wes, "You probably wouldn't be a world champion if you didn't have this birth defect. Be glad you have it." Wes now a freshman and on the United States World Powerlifting team. The coach has taken something and twisted it and made it a positive. But he doesn't look at Wes with any kind of disability. He doesn't have those glasses on at all.

When we found out that Wes had a birth defect and they said what his limitations were going to be—basically contact sports—his father and I just decided it wasn't a hard decision for us. We're raising him just like we would if he didn't have a birth defect. We weren't going to raise him any differently except for the fact that he couldn't play football and he couldn't wrestle. Everything else to us he would be able to do like anybody else. But the hard part was that because we were raising him to be what we thought was normal, other people in the world didn't look at him as normal. It's motherly strength instead of giving in and letting that birth defect rule his life. A lot of parents I know with kids with Klippel-Feil Syndrome felt like bad parents.

Female [White]
Age at report: 65–74
Years of reference: 1960's

Sister Superior switched my roommate three times without my consent in one year just as I started to make friends with my roommates.

I was born with crossed eyes (strabismus), had surgeries at 18 months and at 4 years old, and wore glasses from 14 months. That was the main thing that attracted children's cruelty. As a cross-eyed girl, my darkest moments were on the playground. I could neither hit nor catch a ball, and my schoolmates mocked me for that, loudly. Boys bullied me and broke my glasses at the bus stop, so my parents got a sweet high school girl who lived on our road to ride the bus with me.

At a Christian (Seventh-day Adventist) day school, I was a target of teachers' cruelty because 1) my father refused to say on the school's application that he "believed in the Bible," instead saying he "believed in God," and 2) my parents would not teach me to recite the 23rd Psalm or buy me my own Bible until the school allowed me to learn how to read.

At Episcopal convent school, my Greek teacher was the chaplain (several years later fired for sexual misconduct), who after translations had been finished would turn to me with a leering grin and ask when he would get to hear my confession. (My family was low church, and he was Anglo-Catholic.) I would just look back at him in silence thinking, NEVER. I dreaded that moment in Greek class every day, first class of the day, Grade 9. Sister Superior switched my roommate three times without my consent in one year just as I started to make friends with my roommates. As a cross-eyed girl I was so hungry for friendship and so homesick at age 13. This was devastating! Looking back, I see this as spirit-breaking and cruel. I believe it affected me deeply. I was silent in the face of the cruelty, but clear with my parents and myself that I had been wronged. They were loving champions, but made me stay at the awful schools.

Female, [White]
Age at report: 20
Years of reference: 2000's

I couldn't read it and the teacher made some boy come up and help me, but he was like whispering to me the whole time how stupid I was.

Basically, what happened with me was I took all the tests to try to put me in placement with a learning disability or something like that. And nothing was really coming up. And they took an IQ test and they were like "Oh, she's really intelligent but we can't get her into these resource classes because she's like right on the cusp of needing help and not needing help." So, I was in and out of resource classes. But, of course, when I was in them I did better.

My parents would go twice a week and like chat with the principal like try to get [resources for me]. They did tons of outside tests for me to try to just figure out what it is. Actually, we probably figured it out recently because my little sister was having the same issues and my dad does work with the American Optometric Association. He does HIPAA compliance stuff like that and he met with this one doctor who he was just talking to her about me and my younger sister and she was like," I know exactly what's up." So, bringing the younger one in because she still can't read and she was like 12 by this point. They brought her [my sister] and it turns out she has this thing called convergence excess where your eyes don't work together. They work individually and it causes words when you see them to look like either like a mouse or just like you can read big words but not little words. It's a very like weird thing but it's corrected with like these special types of glasses and vision therapy.

I would always get pulled out of class for tests or just to talk to different teachers or because I couldn't understand something. I would get overwhelmed and I would need to leave the room. And because of that people started to pick on me and make fun of me and I was bullied a lot as a child and that definitely messed up the whole school thing. I remember I have a terrible fear of public speaking and it all started at this exact moment—it started because I was doing a speaking presentation and I couldn't read what I wrote down. My parents wrote it with me and I couldn't read it and the teacher made some boy come up and help me, but he was like whispering to me the whole time how stupid I was. And I was like "I'm not stupid, I just can't read this." I think I was 7 or 8. I realized that I wasn't as dumb as I thought I was. I could actually do things and that I actually understood a lot of what people were saying and I just wasn't giving myself a chance to understand because I just automatically put myself down.

Female [White]
Age at report: 18–25
Years of reference: 2000-2017

Maybe it was because I knew there was no hope; I felt destined for failure and that nothing great would ever be curated from my skills, personality, or life in general.
  I vividly remember being a very joyful and carefree child until around fourth grade. I don't know what happened (I am still trying to pick apart my brain to try and recover the memories) to cause me to feel so anxious and emotionally beat. In fifth to eighth grade I struggled with my weight, going from being very average to the cusp of being morbidly obese. I never was made fun of—at least not that I knew of. I was in on the popular crowd because I was in honors math throughout middle school. Aside from my own internal emotional struggles, I was never able to focus. My darkest moment was asking to use the restroom after my third period math class. I snuck a pair of scissors off the teacher's desk and put them in the waistband of my kilt. I proceeded to feel extremely numb—I couldn't understand exactly why I kept walking. Maybe it was because I knew there was no hope; I felt destined for failure and that nothing great would ever be curated from my skills, personality, or life in general. Anyways, I continued on walking to the second-floor bathroom. I knew no one ever used it. I pushed the heavy wooden door in and I stood in front of the ceiling-to-floor mirror and I didn't recognize the body that was being reflected back. I turned, walked my way into the third stall and… I always gave in to the temptation to sin. I'll forever be a sinner—always choosing the wrong over the right. I always let my anxiety get the best of me. I still continue to let my body dysmorphia eat me alive. Other than self-harming throughout fifth grade to my senior year in high school, I dipped into drugs. I would skip school and go hang out by myself at my favorite places. I started smoking cigarettes my sophomore year of high school. I then moved on to weed shortly afterwards and then dabbled in a few others. It was mainly stealing liquor, getting stoned, and smoking cigarettes. I got a job to keep me out of the house. The only thing that alleviated it was to get stoned or drunk. I pushed everyone away. I'm not entirely sure I ever got over this suffering. I do not smoke cigarettes anymore—I don't drink alcohol anymore. I still struggle to deal with my anxiety and paranoia—I still feel like I failed my parents. I think we never get over suffering—we either just get better

at coping or disguising it behind fake smiles. I really didn't want to go on. I tried various times to end it all, and each time I hung on by a mere piece of fiber. I feel foolish sometimes wishing that my last attempt worked, but now as I have made friendships and have experienced more of the world, I'm so glad it didn't work.

Female [White]
Age at report: 45–54
Years of reference: 1970–1980's

I was overweight in my childhood. I was teased quite a bit about this. Also, I was a high-track student with a learning-disabled younger brother which caused both of us issues. My darkest moment was when my boyfriend broke up with me right before senior prom. I started hanging out with some rough kids. They had me try smoking pot for the first time. I fell prey to the experimentation because nothing seemed to bother them. I made this observation when I really wanted to not be bothered by my recent breakup. The pot smoking made me passive. I struggled with a "less than" self-image. I did not think of my school as a place to find compassion.

Female [White]
Age at report: 20
Years of reference: 2000's-2010's

I got bullied a lot ever since middle school. I'm of a smaller stature and I'm just a small person in general. So, I got teased a lot for my height. People would use me as an armrest—they think it's funny—they used to pass me around and play a game called "Pass the Midget" where they picked me up and tossed me to someone else. People used to come up to me all the time and say "You need to go home and eat more cupcakes because you're too small" things of that nature—always saying like "Oh, can you pick this up…? Can you do this…?" Which influenced me to like stand up for myself and say "Oh, I'm going to go on the track team and throw javelin to prove to you that I am strong." It was mostly about how I looked back in middle school. It was like really anything [them] saying like "Oh, you don't have a boyfriend… you don't have this…." Like middle school kind of teasing. I once got hit upside the head with a pencil case in seventh grade, and in eighth grade someone spread a rumor about me on our trip to Gettysburg. It was a 3-day trip to Gettysburg and someone spread a rumor where I lost all of my friends except for one. Even my brother believed it because he didn't get to see me until the very end of it where I had to tell him "Like, listen this isn't true." It was a rumor that I kicked a girl out who I was rooming with or something stupid like that…. [Now] I have some sort of an eating disorder which I'm in recovery for. I was in an underweight BMI status for all of high school… because I just wasn't eating a lot. I wasn't sleeping a lot…. [The teasing] it took a toll on me physically. But I didn't pay attention to that when I was in high school…I was just very small. And I'm like "Oh, this is just who I am." I was working out a lot to prove I'm strong and stuff and it definitely took a toll on me. And they believe that I had some sort of restrictive eating disorder. I definitely struggle with self-confidence about how I look and stuff like that. I really am tiny and I actually go to the counseling center about anxiety and self-confidence issues. And that's because of a lot of issues focused on the self-confidence body image kind of thing. I do struggle with it because of everything that was said to me for the longest time.

Male [White]
Age at report: 35–44
Years of reference: 1990's

In general, I was the geeky thin kid who wasn't athletic and on top of that had balance and eye issues related to a complicated delivery. In short, I was perceived as being odd at best. This was coupled with my non-traditional thinking style. I liked to find connections between subjects and look at concepts from different points of view in order to fully grasp them. The combination of my physical issues and unique perception caused many a classmate and even teachers to cast me off as a burden to either be pitied or ignored.

Female [White]
Age at report: 20
Years of reference: 2000's–2010's

The whole sticks and stones can break your bones or worse never hurt me is like the biggest lie ever.
    When we entered middle school and sixth grade I was more developed than the other girls physically. It made me more self-conscious than I already was. And, of course, you know people notice and they of course have to say something, right? So, it was very distressing. I did talk to the counselor about it and stuff and she helped me some. I had a counselor outside of school that my mom took me to start seeing. When I got my period and everything, and nobody else had it because I got it really early. I was only like, I was only like 12 and everybody else didn't have it. And you know I really live in a small place where everybody knows your business. And they always have something to say. And then it got a little bit better once everybody started to get it and then everyone was like OK. But then in eighth grade, again, my chest started to grow bigger than the other girls. And we had a dance, a special dance, like a fancy dance, so I went and got a dress and I was all excited to go. And then my teacher was taking pictures so obviously I was in them. And she made a slide show. I guess, like this part [points to cleavage] of my dress was hanging down a little bit so you could see "more than…" Everybody started laughing. And the one boy in my class said "Well, we had a lot to talk about at lunch today." And it just really hurt me.

I went home and I talked to my mom and my grandma about it. You know I threatened to do some things [to myself]. So, my grandma called the school and she complained. And she said to me "I'm not going to lie to you, you do have a big chest for someone your age." She said, "It's nothing." She said, "That's the way you are." And she said "They had no right to do, to do what they did." She said "It was very mean." I mean it still hurts a little bit but now being 21 everybody is, you know. It's not just as bad now. My chest is still big and that I mean it is what it is. Do I still get upset about it? Yeah. If I find a shirt that I like and I can't fit into it you know I cry and like I get all upset about it. But, I think it's not distressing to talk about it anymore. But I mean it brings up some memories...

I don't think we had enough awareness of what bullying can do. The whole sticks and stones can break your bones or worse never hurt me is like the biggest lie ever. Because I would have rather them like punched me than that. I know to this day it really hasn't gotten any better because we had a few kids actually commit suicide because of bullying and they say "You know you need to tell us... you need to tell us." But you tell them and they don't, they don't do anything. They say they do but it doesn't count.

Male, student [White]
Age at report: 47
Years of reference: 1980's

I think it was the teacher's pernicious good intentions. I don't care at all about good intentions. Good intentions that often turn out to have bad outcomes are usually a result of mindlessness.

For all the humiliating experiences that were heaped upon me at home and at school (at home it was school-related) I knew that I could do whatever it was that was being asked of me, but I had a fear of failure. I was reclusive and in part because there were things that I wanted to learn and practice. Shutting the door to my bedroom and being able to do those things were an absolute necessity. But report cards would come in and they were Cs and Ds with a little sprinkling of Fs. I looked at things in terms of what I had to do. For example, when I really picked up music at age 16.

I remember my mom would explain over and over again that school didn't challenge me. She would say school didn't interest my intellect. And moreover, she said there's nothing there that elicits my creativity and my imagination. My mother tried to persuade my father that I wasn't an underachiever. For her, that was too simplistic. I was reading literary classics one after another. I was practicing music for hours a day with an attitude. I was learning music and drawing. I drew from imagination. I remember my mother said, "He's not drawing roses and skulls or any of that cliché stuff." I set forth my own curriculum at a very young age.

The heart of the school stuff: I was a dummy. I was stupid. I was hopeless dah, dah dah, on one hand; but by my senior year in high school my peers were telling me that I was brilliant. So, my stepmom really seized upon me, she was unrelenting and around 16 years old there were very serious mixed messages coming in. She would call me stupid, lazy, irresponsible, mentally deranged. She took my early drawings to the school psychologist and would call me a dummy, a recluse and said I was angry. She would tell everybody around the orbit of our household that I had anger problems. She said I had all this anger built up in me, when in fact I did not. In fact, I was just reclusive and in part because there were things I wanted to learn and practice.

In first grade a teacher gathered us around her because she was going to tell us a story. She told a story about a shy kid who keeps his hand in his pocket. It turns out the boy in the story is me. She called me to the front and had me raise my highly deformed right hand to the class. It was devastating. I was 5 years old. I think it was the teacher's pernicious good intentions. I don't care at all about good intentions. Good intentions that often turn out to have bad outcomes are usually a result of mindlessness. Those outcomes are usually a result of not taking the time and the effort to reflect upon how those "good intentions" might make others feel. That was the first of many awful things.

It was a desultory experience. And emerged as part of my incipient understanding of being put on display. It was an understanding that not only was I different, but I was deformed. There was a certain ugliness about me. It made me feel ugly; that I was grotesque like a carnival attraction. I did tell my mother. She went to the school, and I remember the teacher being absolutely terrified—petrified.

This incident contributed to an ongoing paranoia narrative where I believe that I was a miscarriage survivor, that I was a blight upon nature and a mistake. All of nature wanted me dead. And even when I first went to school I thought of school as punishment. And for a while I thought my parents and my teachers were colluding to kill me. That narrative has stayed with me because I have recurrent cancer. I feel like a mistake of nature.

When I got into eighth grade and onto high school those were hard times. I went to extreme lengths to have my deformed hand in my pocket. Sometimes I would fake an injury and have it in a sling or carry a backpack in a way that covered my hand. There were so many involuntary trips to the school psychologist. Schoolmarms would just barge in, interrupt the class, collect me for the psychologist but always announce why they were there and where I was going.

I started to feel threatened like I was being hunted. It really revved up the paranoia. That was a whole new level of anxiety. It was about four or five trips to the school psychologist and my peers began to see me as you got some weird problems—not just the hand, but he's weird. Those first years of high school were absolute misery. There were people who would recoil from a handshake, and there were (mostly) girls who actually leapt away in disgust and fear from my hand. It's not a good feeling to be perceived as grotesque. School and its K through 12, it's screwed up.

VIII *Struggles with Learning*

Female, school principal [Black]
Age at report: 47
Years of reference: Late 70's –80's

I suffered from a lack of exposure, low-level vocabulary development, poor writing skills, [and] not enough parent/family participation. Not having the skills to complete or even begin a task, not having the supports needed from the adults at school or home, afraid to ask for help, letting people know how much help was really needed, the feeling of being alone and worried. [I also had] difficulty making and keeping good friends.

Female, student [White]
Age at report: 26
Years of reference: 2010's

Junior year of high school I got really depressed. I don't really know why but my grades did drop then and I didn't do so well. Math, my grades overall kind of struggled, with math was like my major issue. It was just I struggled to get up in the morning and do the work and focus in school. The teachers were all very supportive and I was in drumline at the time and that I also had a teacher. My English teacher was the drumline person and he came up with a program for me to have my teachers sign that I did all the work that I needed. He was restructuring and helped me. Because if I didn't do all the work, I wasn't allowed to be in drumline. And that was like a big important thing to me. I really enjoyed it [and it] was like the one happy thing I had going on at the time. So that helped me kind of like re-motivate myself and like brought my grades back up. I was able to stay in drumline.

Female [White]
Age at report: 26–34
Years of reference: 2000's-2010's

In elementary school, I remember struggling with math. As I continued to struggle with math, my grades began to slip. I ended up having to seek tutoring which became embarrassing for a young student my age. At times I would try to avoid studying or completing math assignments that were too difficult for me because they would cause me upset and I would not want to think about it.

Female [White]
Age at report: 35–44
Years of reference: 1980's

My biggest issues were with figuring out math in seventh grade. My brothers were all really good at math, and I just did not understand why I struggled so much. My parents tried to help but they were as lost about algebra as I was. I had to seek help with after-school time at the Math Clinic. I was a very good student and was "tracked" in high-achieving classes so to be in a class where I did not understand the lessons and concepts was scary and frustrating. Plus knowing that my peers seemed to all be able to do it so easily was embarrassing.

My darkest moment was being called on to put a problem on the board and standing there forever and trying to get the right answer. I did not get it right, and I distinctly remember the sting of embarrassment as my teacher had to correct what I had put on the board. I wanted to sink into the floor!

I put the pressure on myself and made it a point that I was going to figure this algebra out or die trying! The Math Clinic ran on certain days after school. I had to stay probably 2–3 times a week after school to work on my homework there. It was frustrating that it took me so much longer to figure problems but eventually I caught on and everything "clicked" for me.

Female [White]
Age at report: 26–34
Year of reference: 2009

I was asked to read aloud for the class. The teacher then interrupted me and asked to me to stop reading. After class the teacher pulled me aside and suggested further testing for my reading ability. The test scores showed that I was just below average. I was put into a specialized reading class that was a level lower than the average student. I felt belittled and dumb. The new teacher had treated me like I was not able to read at all, when in fact it was just that I had difficulty comprehending what I read. Yes it's paralyzing. I do not read. I do not and attempt to read books for pleasure, although I enjoy going to bookstores. It has hindered my success.

Female [White]
Age at report: 18–24
Years of reference: 2000's–2010's

For me, I was not very "school-oriented" and I went to a college prep high school, which means it was hard. I didn't study as much as I should have and I could have done better. When applying to colleges and SAT's came around, I was a little behind. And it got a little worse for me when I didn't get into the school I wanted to and my other classmates were getting into amazing schools that I could never think about getting into. I would say that determination in school and the want to put the work in was hard for me. I think not getting into my top choice school was very hard for me and it took a toll on me as well. It was hard seeing everyone get into the schools that they wanted to and then there was me who had to settle for less and that was my own fault.

IX *Solicitude*

Female [Hispanic]
Age at report: 26–34
Years of reference: 1990's

As a child, school didn't come easy to me. I had to study hard to even just pass. I needed a lot of reviewing which wasn't always allowed and at times it was embarrassing. As I got older, I was able to find different strategies to help keep up and get better grades. Today, my son has this same problem, and has been diagnosed with ADHD. It has been a huge struggle for him to keep up. It breaks my heart hearing him suffer through the same things I did. My darkest moment in school isn't really mine, but something I witnessed happen to someone else in school. In my junior high school, we shared extracurricular classes, such as art and music, with special needs kids. I remember one time in my art class, there was a special needs boy who must have been having a bad day, or a particularly hard time with this art project. He was very upset and was making "weird" noises and gestures. Some kids were getting annoyed by this. One decided to start yelling at the boy. They were complaining and didn't know why we needed to share classes with "retards" anyway. They were being extremely mean. That only made things worse and the special needs boy got louder and more frustrated. Eventually they had to take him out of the classroom to calm him down. I remember feeling so bad for the boy. I know he must have understood even a little bit of what the other person was saying about him and to him. And other kids who were more verbal but still special needs definitely understood. It broke my heart. And for what? The disrespectful kid didn't even get in trouble. The teacher just reprimanded them and said it was wrong.

Male [White]
Age at report: 18–25
Years of reference–2000's–2010's

What makes me feel pain is the time gone by and knowing that some of those people I'll never see again such as teachers, students, and family. I can remember how a kid a grade above me committed suicide the one day over the weekend and we found out that Monday. I didn't really know the kid but I felt like it was such a great waste to have life and now it's gone. Everything he could have accomplished will never be in this world or reality. Sometimes I get depressed and sad but this again is brought on by life and the memories that I've had knowing that I can never go back and see the people who once were alive, but it only hurts because I've gotten to have these memories.

Female, parent [White]
Age at report: 55–64
Years of reference: 2000's

Looking at your survey brought me to a pause as I realized how much pain and despair it made me feel. I have managed not to give too much power to the way other people view me in my life, following my mother's advice that "People only have the power on you that you give them," to which I have added, "What people think of me is none of my business." But it is a different matter when it concerns my children, and it still hurts to think of how students in Stuart's kindergarten classroom singled him out for his weaknesses and ganged against him like a wounded animal to be killed. Stuart performed poorly due to his dyslexia and had asocial behaviors such as gas-passing from his lactose intolerance. As a teenager, Stuart learned to hide his physical and mental weaknesses, but he was often the target for a group of children to abuse him as a child. Years later, it still fills me with a rage I never experienced otherwise, akin to a primal female impulse to protect her baby at any cost.

I was surprised that you asked about the brightest moment of the school experience as a conclusion. Something in me refused to go that way, but understand you would hope that we managed to stitch our suffering experiences into something beautiful. You mention Columbine. One thing striking about massacres is how when some people act in horrific ways, there are always others who respond in heroic ways. For example, during the Virginia Tech massacre, one teacher was a Holocaust survivor who had wondered his whole life why he got to live while so many died. When the shooter came down the hallway, he made his students jump through a window to safety while holding the door closed as long as he could. He saved many of them, and as he died, I like to think that he received the answer to his question.

Likewise, some teachers have the impulse to protect children and take the bullet for them, sometimes literally when they jump in front of them. When the children are very young, I imagine teachers gathering their students in death, comforting and helping them find their dead grandparents or ancestors, and remaining with them as long as needed. It comforts me as well.

So, what did we do to help our Stuart? I was a classroom mom, and the next time I went to his classroom to read a story…no, I did not punch the children, even though I thought about it. Instead, I look at them in the eyes, pausing at each one of them, hoping to reach their soul. My husband also came on his own, and we made the teacher aware of the situation in the most tactful way possible. We don't know what she did, but a few days later, Stuart came home happy because a boy had offered him to play with two of them at the playground, and when the third boy started to complain, he stood up for Stuart. The boy was from Eastern Europe, and his dad worked with the CDC for a couple of years. One friend is enough to make a difference, and I'll always be grateful to him for changing the tide. He was a hero and willing to take a bullet for Stuart.

The last month of school was much better, and we looked for a private school specializing in learning disabilities. My husband told me later that if we had not found one, he would have campaigned for me to homeschool Stuart until we found one that would be safe for him.

References

Schohaus, W. (2012/1932). *The dark place of education: with a collection of seventy-eight reports of school experiences*. Routledge.

Spinoza, B. (1677). *Tractatus politicus*.

6 Interpretations and Discussion

Education is necessarily always full of problems. It should adjust itself to Life. But the outward manifestations of life are subject to constant change, and therefore constant alterations must take place both in the internal and external organization of the schools.

(Schohaus, 2012/1932, p. 333)

We open with this quote from Schohaus to draw attention to the "subject of constant change". Schohaus's (2012/1932) insights about schooling and the experiences of children during his time led him to the prescient acknowledgment that schools must and will change. The institution, both internally and externally, needs to "adjust itself to Life". Our work follows from his—in a different time and place—but it is the same institution with different "outward manifestations of life". What has changed, and what remains the same with respect to those "dark places"?

Schohaus (2012/1932) presented an involved conceptual analysis prior to the organization of actual reports by his participants. Here we take the opposite approach and offer insights about our categorization and the meanings held for student suffering, how schools and those who work in them are implicated, and possibilities for a path forward.

"Suffering is the subversive voice in the biomedical discourse; it is central among all things that do not fit" (Frank, 1992, p. 360). We argue the same here: that suffering is the subversive voice in the education discourse. The voice is central among all things that do not fit, yet it confronts the people who inhabit the school nevertheless. We've learned that suffering is a constant in schools, yet rarely is it identified as such. It quietly exists in classrooms, hallways, the schoolyard, teachers' lounge and offices, and across schools' and students' social realms. Suffering has been part of schooling for ages, singularly and systematically.

Sadness, despair, lament, anger, frustration, loneliness, hopelessness, and disappointment are just some of the emotions that make up suffering. There are different occasions in life where and when these emotions occur. Here we learn they are, unfortunately, closely tied to school. It is clear from the narratives and our own lives that, for many of us, negative emotions are simply hard to work out. They are challenging to withstand and to prevail over. Although

DOI: 10.4324/9780429465499-6

reports in Chapter 5 do not tell this story, many participants overcame the most difficult situations and proved a personal resolve that became a certain resilience. For others, feelings of loss or disappointment have remained, perhaps forever. But it is not about the overcoming of suffering, or the succumbing to it in sum—it is the fact that what occurred happened in school. And yet, it is still difficult to understand a sufferer's totality of emotions when their stories are gathered together. It is their treatment that forever evokes an emotional response. The narratives exclaim, "I am angry at being overlooked, at being ignored". Students were made to feel inferior; they were handled, denigrated, degraded, forgotten, processed, and hurt along the way. In many instances, a particular mode of the professionally efficient regarded student suffering as merely a temporary disturbance. What remains is the saddening realization that "things could have been otherwise".

We categorized participant reports into nine themes that reflect the contemporary suffering students experience in schools. Our categorization is provided for the reader only as current parallels to Schohaus's (2012/1932) groupings. It is vital to highlight that categorization ultimately obscures the ontology, the personhood, the face of the school experience of suffering. Because what is valued is prioritized, we believe orienting empathetically to the causes of suffering in schools is equally, if not more, foundational to the formation of an educational leader than is understanding isolated and narrow practice issues such as trauma-informed instruction, social and emotional education, or tiered response to intervention. Although all practice elements must function hand in hand to build an ethical school (Starratt, 1991) and deliver on what is owed students against all else (Spillane & Lowenhaupt, 2019), empathy brought forth from a keen awareness of the human condition, we believe, comes first.

Affront to Personhood/Injury to Dignity

Imperviousness to student and parent requests. Denial of simple needs and wishes. Trivializing basic human rights. Dishonoring and/or openly disrespecting. Dignity is an existential value about personhood in its various dimensions—physical, psychological, and social. This implies that personhood constitutes an integrity or wholeness. When this is threatened, existence itself is threatened. "Viewed this way, indignity is the effacement of personhood" (Addis, 2019, p. 323).

Anxiety, Stress, and Fear

Fear of giving presentations, speaking in class, taking tests, school schedules, and the like. Students are vulnerable and, at times, fear their teachers and other students. There is stress when the school shows disorder due to short staffing. There is fear of the unknown and the uncontrollable, such as bomb threats and the confusion that ensues. Fear is what students experience when they feel a threat from the outside; anxiety is a threat from inside their own consciousness (Cox, 2021). Conversely, Kierkegaard (1980/1844) concludes that "Whoever has learned to be anxious in the right way, has learned the ultimate" (p. 155).

Companionship and Isolation

Students lack skill in making and keeping friends. They were abandoned by their peers, picked on by teachers (sometimes for no reason at all, or because of an oddity or precociousness), and left lonely and confused to survive by their own devices. Schohaus (2012/1932) noted that in school "happiness gained from youthful friendships stands as a focal point" (p. 90). Yet, as he also discovered, the nature of school cultures and the giving of grades "manifests the spirit of rivalry" and hinders the process of making friends leading "to the necessity of every child seeking his own personal advancement, his personal success before anything else" (p. 93).

Personal, Cultural, and Social Identity

Students suffered discrimination by school staff, teachers, and their peers because of their race, gender, sexuality, religion, and ethnicity. Although not exclusively, students from vulnerable, minoritized, and other identities outside the status quo suffered because they were not protected by school policies or practices. Staff failed to carry out inclusive visions and related missions respectful to all students and their families. Students suffered because of the differences between the magnanimity of what is promised and what is delivered, the ease of what is perceived as normally granted to others versus the truculence required on their part to receive necessary academic and social supports. The types of social provision found to be lacking in schools for students who suffered because of their personal, cultural, or social identity include emotional, appraisal, instrumental, informational, and policy supports (Day et al., 2020; Muñoz-Plaza et al., 2002).

Lateral Violence, Bullying and Discrimination

Students who suffered because of lateral violence experienced gossip, shaming, backstabbing, social exclusion, physical violence, and varying levels of physical and emotional abuse. They experienced bullying by teachers and peers. Schools did not provide adequate consequences to the perpetrator for the damage done, nor rectify the conditions that allowed the behavior to continue. Sometimes suffering occurred and there was little a student could do, as the context or situation allowed or tolerated it, or the person who perpetrated the bullying was protected. The effects of bullying on victims and perpetrators are well documented. Bullying victimization is associated with delinquent behavior; significantly greater internalizing of problems; the highest levels of physical or psychosomatic health problems; an increased risk for suicidal ideation and suicidal/self-harm behavior; manifestation of poor school adjustment; and more negative perceived school climate (Wolke and Lereya, 2015).

Educator Indiscretion, Impropriety, and Transgression

Students sustained verbal, emotional, and physical abuse due to teachers acting cruelly, inhumanely, and unethically toward them. Withstanding classroom climates of emotional abuse, they were physically hit or paddled, verbally berated and abused for not responding quickly enough or knowing an answer. Students were cruelly punished for defending another student, isolated for their learning needs, disciplined by humiliation, ostracized for their personal characteristics, and/or made victims of outright favoritism. Some experienced sexual grooming and sexual assault with no consequences to the offender. When reported, there were instances when the victim was not believed and was further humiliated. All these incidents are also affronts to a student's dignity and personhood. Conduct went unreported (normally out of fear) or was undetected. All caused lasting disassociation, humiliation, and shame. As Harber has noted (2004), in reality the situation is direr than depicted in accounts reporting that formal schooling has been directly violent to both learners and the wider society. It commonly goes unaddressed that school cultures often allow the cruel treatment of children, and directly contribute to violence in society. "Reference in the press to violence in schools is most commonly about pupil to pupil or pupil to teacher violence … rarely is the role of the school itself seen as problematic in any systematic way" (pp. 1–2).

Corporeal Disaffection/Physicality

Students, both abled and disabled, suffered because of their natural physical shape and/or size, including their height, weight, or congenital disability. Students experienced cruel and degrading treatment from peers and teachers, were treated unfairly or discriminated against, and were not granted opportunities other students were. Although "corporeal dissatisfaction may be a normative condition in all societies and at all times", corporeal *disaffection* and disorder instigated by the culture and climate of schooling is something different. "[T]he cocktail of high performance mixed with body centered pathology codes … may have deeply damaging consequences for students' identity, their education and health, particularly for those emotionally vulnerable and at risk" (Evans et al., 2008, pp. 399–400).

Struggles with Learning

Students struggled through their lessons (particularly in math, but other subjects, too), oftentimes even with the necessary supports to learn what was set out. Students suffered from a lack of exposure to subject areas beyond the basics and poor pedagogical practice that failed students at the most basic and advanced levels. Students agonized because of the use of methods and practices that either lacked engaging elements or required an exactitude on the part of the teacher. The lessons were missing precision and accuracy to meet the needs of individual students. Experiences of disconnection or hostility between the teacher and student caused struggles with learning. Students suffered due to their own attitudes toward learning and the reckoning of not making the grade. All this added to anxiety, feelings of inadequacy, uncertainty, and ridicule from other students. Schohaus (2012/1932) found that "the school does not realize how to construct its work upon the child's natural love of achievement and therefore allows this to become stunted" (p. 46).

Solicitude

Parents suffered because they care for their children and try to prepare them for the challenges in the world. They reported feeling powerless to participate in or control the school environment or influence conditions to their child's advantage. Students and the school did not treat their children fairly or respond adequately to the needs of a situation. Students suffered because they saw others being mistreated at school and were helpless to assist, or they learned of a peer who committed suicide. Solicitude draws people closer to a common shared humanity. "Solicitude, as an ethical relationship, does not expect any recognition of the self by the other. Any movement from the self to the other implies an implicit mutuality that involves giving without expecting a response" (Moreno et al., 2021, pp. 125–126).

Categorical Themes and the Literature

The literature on suffering reviewed in Chapter 3 helps us to understand and further interpret the lifeworld of students. In this section we begin to make sense of the connections between existing literature and our study findings. We have learned that any school event, incident, or experience may give rise to suffering for any particular student. Therein lies the challenge. As with a clinician attempting to heal a patient, an educator working with a suffering student must have the courage to establish relational trust and possess confidence in order to understand and begin to process the circumstances that gave rise to the suffering and provide help. Any students' suffering is subjective, unique, and personal, requiring an interpersonal, multifaceted response that incorporates a sophisticated familiarity with human nature and the ways of the heart.

In a school, biopsychosocially, the alleviation of suffering demands the understanding of a student's social, emotional, physical, and contextual response to what caused them to suffer. Suffering as a student's emotional state, as a *feeling*, rather than an objective, clinical, or pathological analysis or diagnosis, demands a hermeneutic appraisal of the holistic perspective of the student on personal terms (the emotional, phenomenal, and sociocultural) and a clear understanding of the external contextual landscape of the school environment. This is what is required of the educator in order to have empathic understanding and attempt to be in empathetic attunement with the student (Glucksman, 2020; Stiegler et al., 2018; Chapman & Gavrin, 1993; Cassell, 1999). Empathic understanding is "understanding of the possibilities in which we live" (Agosta, 2020). As in healthcare when a clinician first meets their patient, the beginning for an educator is when they encounter the suffering student and ask, "How can I help?" and then reflect, "Who is this other person, [this student in front of me who is suffering], as a possibility?" (Agosta, 2020).

Suffering work as ethereal and existential care is work that requires a delicacy and softness which is not often spoken of in educational leadership. Our realization that existential distress felt at the end of life has similarities to experiences of suffering and anguish students have in school gives us pause. Feelings of meaninglessness, not having a primary role, not being valued by others, feelings of worthlessness and hopelessness, questioning why something has happened to them, and a worry about not meeting expectations or aspirations were all part of participants' narratives. We do not believe we are taking any type of risk in saying that we all can identify with the reports. Laying the landscape of a teacher or administrator in this space requires a deep realization of our shared human vulnerability and a belief in transcendent possibility. In the end, for healing of the suffering student, the work of an educator will require them to bind themselves, the suffering student, and the non-suffering student, all to the same community. All the best aspects of the school environment, all the resources and possibilities available, must be accessible and obtainable so that students may endure and ultimately flourish as a result.

Suffering in school is bound to happen. We all suffer for one reason or another, and as Freud (1930) found, and the narratives attest, students suffer in school because of other people—their peers and those who surrounded them and with whom they interact as a matter of course. Students suffer because they inhabit the world with others and the external world is beyond their control. Our own bodies are sites of suffering, too. As Davies (2012) noted, when a student suffers, it is not always a sign of being disordered, nor a sign of illness, but rather of emotional awareness of the conflicts that arise in response to the differing positions we can take when navigating social reality. Children and youth are often faced with handling very difficult emotions as a matter of course through their schooling. Their ability to understand difficult emotions, and having the means to process them both directly and vicariously, help to form a simple, grounded sturdiness that aids in the growth of compassion toward self and others (Weisz & Zaki, 2017).

Plainly, dependent upon the system of school a student is subject to, as each grade is a separate encounter, students become accustomed to the ways of that system. Over time, the system begins to serve a particular type of student, one who is in line with the goals, aims, and ambitions of that system. If a student does not fit that mold, the conditions prove stultifying because the student's curiosity, interests, and hence full potential are not being addressed by the system. A student (or their parents) resisting or attempting to change the system for themselves, which requires interacting and advocating, brings about suffering—evident in isolation, confusion, or conflicts with peers, teachers and/or school staff.

Suffering also arises in predictable ways around student growth. As a student goes through school, they find their internal world, both physical and metaphysical, to be out of step with the external world they inhabit. New interests such as excelling in sports, the arts, or academics; ideas such as how society addresses race, gender, sexuality, and ethnicity; the experience of some life-changing event at home, such as a divorce, remarriage, or a sick sibling—all require navigation and negotiation of new and old ideas and relationships. This struggle between a student's internal growth and their relationship with the external world is commonly the plotline of *bildungsroman* novels in literature classes around the world. Suffering in school through adolescence is more common than we think.

A student will suffer because they realize that there is a problem but do not yet understand that problem fully. Without a proper education on the ways of suffering, students will seek to anesthetize themselves from suffering through drugs, alcohol, and other escapist avenues that do not address understanding, but serve as only a temporary alleviation of the suffering. It is an education *par excellence* that informs us about the causes of human suffering, and that such suffering is a natural response to external conditions we are trying (and struggling) to relate to.

From a psychological perspective, the literature points out that a suffering student's silent lament is unique and personal. Knowing that "their internal tendencies are frustrated" (van Hooft, 2000, p. 179), we should aim to catch an important glimpse of that uniqueness, which we can highlight in our suffering work with the student, emphasizing that "hidden away somewhere a secret life [exists] that is satisfactory because of it being creative or original to that human being" (Winnicott, 1971, p. 68). Carefully seeing into that secret life, with humility, requires a certain heroism that is equivalent to "compassionate action at the risk of personal sacrifice" (Zimbardo et al., 2017).

Some participant reports intimate or reveal outright that students found solace for their suffering in either the ritualistic, contemplative, or dogmatic nature of religion. For others, religion played no part in helping them in their suffering. Realized more narrowly by students, and a cause of great confusion and stress, was the inexplicable nature of their suffering; they did not comprehend that suffering was not a consequence of some fault of theirs. Suffering happens as a matter of life; conceivably, the idea is to simply understand better, and perhaps ultimately realize the only meaning that suffering can have is that it teaches us to care for others (Van Hooft, 1998). To alleviate suffering, humans must act. It is as much a call to practical action and moral duty as it is an existential and spiritual one. The same applies to the one suffering as well as to the one who is positioned to heal. Suffering is a place of spiritual promise and the potential for mending and healing. Trusting through faith provides a deep well of resources to encourage a suffering student to overcome and feel connected to others in a spiritual community. "Religious and spiritual perspectives provide a context in which such understanding can take place in seeing suffering as an invitation to growth in character or as an invitation to turn to God" (Vanderweele, 2019, p. 64).

With schools being on the receiving end of an unjust society, it follows that there are economic, political, and social factors that cause suffering in schools (Fullan, 2019); these, overall, are beyond the scope of this study. For example, the persistence of corporal punishment, draconian immigration policies, and racial disparities exacerbated by the culture wars all impact and provide ample instigation for suffering in schools.

From Perpetrating Suffering to Complicity in Suffering

There is a dual message communicated by Schohaus (2012/1932) in his concluding analysis of the schools of his time. The entire volume serves not only as an exposé of "important inadequacies of…schools in matters of great urgency" (p. 15) but as a clear indictment against the treatment of children by the schooling process itself. Particularly, the denunciations focus on operational and pedagogical approaches that resulted in direct harm to students in the form of corporal punishment, contempt, overt partiality, "sitting still hour after hour," shaming, repetitive rote learning, limiting of social interaction and friendship, denial of children as fully human, generalized lack of understanding, lack of affection, and the list goes on.

Yet in his final analysis, Schohaus (2012/1932) retains a faith in the increasingly humane possibilities of schooling. He speaks of "the new school" and how it will manifestly become "a place of intensive and happy development of life" (p. 100). Although pragmatic in the sense that every nation deserves the kind of education it has, he clearly holds the position that "as a whole schools are not bad, but they could be much, much better" (p. 333). To level blame on many fronts for the inadequacies of schools, and particularly for the one-sided technocratic success in the emergence of organized mass schooling, yet hold a deep faith in the ideal of schooling where "everything possible will be done lovingly to confirm young people in all their impulses for life and development" resulting in provision for "a free, happy, and strong existence" (p. 337) takes an enormous vision. Schohaus (2012/1932), informed by his present, was able to see a future that we, in tandem with him, wish to honor and speak into.

Our assessment of schooling based on the reports of suffering rendered in this book is to conclude, as Schohaus (2012/1932) did, that we certainly can do much, much better. Clearly, there have been organizational and pedagogical improvements with an ever-increasing awareness of the varied needs and interests of students who make claims against the schools and educators (Worsfold, 1980), but this does not necessarily systematically reach to the heart of professional formation and the development of dispositions of those who act directly or indirectly upon children. In this sense, schools of today are more complicit in the suffering of students, rather than perpetrating harm in direct ways. One of the reports is illustrative of this pervasive unconsciousness, an uncritical relationality adopted by teachers and manifested as blind indifference when responding to the unique and varied needs of students. Good intentions that often turn out to have bad outcomes are usually a result of mindlessness. Those good intentions are pernicious for the very fact that the profession must be formed, committed to, and guided by a thoroughgoing praxis. Schohaus (2012/1932) was prescient about this when he makes an assertion about the need for an "educational understanding" that is a "sharp-sighted love for all the good possibilities which as yet lie dormant within the character of children" (p. 76). With any careful reading of the reports in Chapter 5 it becomes obvious that praxis continues to remain a challenge for realizing an even better "new school".

Suffering's Continuum

Our decision to conduct this study never brought to mind the evaluation or measurement of suffering that our participants experienced. Devising a continuum to measure the degree of suffering our participants felt from anxiety around testing to threats to their personhood because of significant bullying was not our goal. We believe that doing so could have potentially degraded our commitment to what had been shared and how we conceived the study. On the whole, the reports reveal a range of healthy as well as dangerous suffering and evidence of creative and uncreative responses. There is worth in this evaluation process for future studies, keeping in mind that the determination of school events or activities and students' suffering in response requires special discernment. Vanderweele (2019) suggests empathetic questions, such as the following, can be used in conversation by a caring leader to help a suffering student express themselves and aid in better understanding and providing relief and assistance:

- To what extent are you suffering?
- How intense is the suffering? Is it tolerable?
- How long have you had these feelings?
- What aspects of your life are particularly impacted due to this suffering?
- Have certain purposes of your life badly disrupted because of what you have been experiencing?
- Do you feel as if what you have been experiencing threatens who you are as a person?

(p. 61)

We believe that if educators are to carry out suffering work, a place to start is with the realization and belief that the existential and the phenomenological exist in school settings, along with the practical, as a precursor to any pathological diagnoses.

Suffering and Moral Injury

Although all suffering is not morally injurious, a substantial amount can be. When we reference moral injury in relation to suffering in schools, we are concerned about the internalization of harm (both actual and perceived) that warps the sensibility, attitude, and outlook of children about the nature of people and organizational systems that contribute to confusion about what is right, true, good, and praiseworthy. A useful operational definition is offered by Drescher et al. (2011) when they explain that moral injury is a disruption of a person's expectation and/or confidence about their own or another's capacity to exhibit moral behavior, manifesting in responses to events that violate that person's moral beliefs—particularly the capacity to behave in just and ethical ways.

As Otte (2015) has suggested, even though moral injury has focused on war veterans and police officers, the construct is relevant for other populations who face morally injurious situations, and this is particularly the case for females. These insights are especially relevant for those who shared school reports with us that appear in Chapter 5, as a large portion of participants were women of all ages. We can see from a wide range of reports that "lasting psychological, biological, spiritual, behavioral, and social impact [occurred by] perpetrating, failing to prevent, or bearing witness to acts that transgress moral beliefs and expectations" (Litz et al., 2009, p. 697).

The reports are replete with children and youth experiencing a range of suffering phenomena that school personnel largely ignored out of indifference, ignorance, operational expediency, or direct offence. *In these cases, students possessed more moral sensibility (evidenced in their injury) than the adults charged with educating them.* This "dark place" of education corresponds with interpretations of Schohaus (2012/1932) almost 100 years ago when it was asserted that "the real purport … pins our attention to things that matter in the school; and things that matter are not so much physical as spiritual" (p. 8).

What the reports give us is a glaring absence of education as soulcraft (Graves & Swain, 2016). They highlight the important hidden curriculum of *inspirit* as expressed through Moffett (2006) and Crawford (2006). Soulcraft is the curricular and pedagogical inspiration of students—schooling that speaks into the fullest possible unique personhood of a learner. We would all agree that schools should be, to the greatest extent possible, places not of moral injury but of repair—places of flourishing and holistic well-being. This rightly calls forth a "pedagogy of engaging with pain and suffering" with an intentional disruption of normalized school practices to facilitate active reconstruction of "soul and spirits for different purposes, ranging from survival and mourning to healing, and in some cases mobilization toward collective-action for personal, and systemic change" (Eizadirad & Sider, 2021, p. 221). In other words, seeing into "the dark corners of existence" and "visibilizing" suffering is necessary to effectively respond with compassion, uplift, and hope (p. 222). This, of course, is "morally serious pedagogy" focused on a range of "aptitudes, commitments, and appetites necessary to achieve the goods at which [schooling] aims, intellectually and otherwise. In short, [schools] cannot neglect [a full] formation of their students" (Floyd, 2010, pp. 265–6).

The Institutionalized School and the Education Workers Who Occupy It

As the institution of schooling interpretively "tinkers toward utopia" (Tyack & Cuban, 1995) there is a distinction to be made between schools and their organizational features and the professional dispositions and orientations of teachers and administrators who work within them. As the global education sector becomes ever-increasingly robust, its full societal impact becomes progressively more apparent (Baker, 2014). Educationally derived human capital significantly influences a nation's economic growth (Hanushek et al., 2022). And as Baker and others demonstrate, education is now a fundamental social variable in demography (Baker, 2014; Baker et al., 2011). Our destiny is the ever-increasing expansion of schooling—adapting, altering, and changing other modern institutions of society. With the robust expansion of schooling and its concomitant reforms, school organizations have adopted a range of technocratic responses and "solutions" to the challenges of expansion and "improvement". We can both read and infer from the reports of students the backdrop of these school settings. They are places characterized by efficiencies, production, uniform approaches to managing and controlling operations, intentionally constructed imbalanced power relations, standards-based accountability testing cultures and a focus on technical determinations rather than close-at-hand adaptive responses to the character and needs of children (Heifetz & Laurie, 2001).

The technical is one thing; the adaptive is entirely another. Schooling continues to improve—technically, although much of this is subject to criticism. But the adaptive becomes paramount for a sector in which the central work is human making. We contend that as students suffer in schools, so can the adults who labor there. With a reliance on organizationally sponsored technical solutions to schooling problems, the humanistic adaptive work of schooling abates—so much so that the orientations of teachers and administrators themselves evidence a loss of a visionary ideal that is intended to bring moral rewards for those who engage and work with children (Santoro, 2011). As with Schohaus's (2012/1932) accounts of the problems of the profession of his time, we detect a range of school worker indifference to the needs of students in ways that can be characterized as goal displacement—attending to other organizational matters as if they were more important than the very students themselves (Bohte & Meier, 2002). Here then is the entry point for some in the profession who have lost a visionary ideal, have become demoralized, suffer in their daily challenges with both the school organization and its children, and unfortunately develop warped sensibilities about the meaning and significance of their supposed calling.

Compassionate schools as sites of human organization can be a space for compassionate workers who in kind are equipped to be compassionate toward learners who may ultimately be compassionate with each other (Driver, 2007; Kanov et al., 2004; Moreno et al., 2021). This calls for dramatic deprogramming and reprogramming in terms of leadership and policy (Nussbaum, 2001). Institutional compassion exists

> when members of a system collectively notice, feel and respond to pain experienced by members (Kanov et al., 2004). Focusing on institutional responses to suffering among its members allows us to understand how collective proactive, creative, and empathetic actions help bind organizations.
>
> (Moreno et al., 2021, p. 609)

The institutionalizing of compassion is based on the inevitable suffering we all can experience in school settings. Policies that are built to encourage responsive and ethical address of suffering and its hoped-for alleviation are part of the important work of remaking the school organization (Kanov et al., 2004). "Compassionate action is a practice, one of the most advanced" (Chödrön, 1997, p. 78). And although it is unlikely to mandate what matters, policies and practices that are aligned to the spirit of compassion will necessitate a collective endeavor toward "an awareness of the suffering (cognitive), a sympathetic concern (affective), a desire to relieve the suffering (intentional), and a readiness to help relieve the suffering (motivational)" (Moreno et al., 2021, p. 609).

A Path Forward

From our analysis we hope to stimulate discussion that leads to improved theorizing and practice within schooling generally and the field of educational leadership particularly. The message contained within the chapters is meant to invoke a response that encapsulates the entire person of the reader. Frick and Covaleskie (2014) emphasize that integrity means the ethical commitments part of one's personal identity will also guide professional practice. Studying suffering in schools necessarily contributes to one's moral literacy and continuously developing ethical commitments (Faircloth, 2021; Frick et al., 2013; Polizzi & Ronan, 2020; Starrat, 2005; Tuana, 2007).

Understanding, discerning, and alleviating suffering in schools form an integral existential component of the ethical practices of school workers and especially those educational leaders charged with setting direction and exercising influence within their respective schools and school systems. A clear call is for educators to realize that the existential and the phenomenological exist in school settings. At the center of an existentialist approach to understanding suffering in schools is its "character as a gesture of protest against academic philosophy, its anti-system sensibility, its flight from the 'iron cage of reason' and rationale" (Crowell, 2020, n.p.). By holding to these descriptions, this approach essentially and unequivocally advocates for dignity and respect for the human person, explores new aspects of human nature, and highlights divergent methods to understand people (Corey, 2011).

As we are calling for a recognition of the existential and phenomenological in the practices of schools and the discipline of school leadership, this study and its focus on suffering raises questions that go beyond the conventional, personal, cultural, and societal to the experiential, considering "what life means and what is at stake in living". Suffering's continuum begins here in the center, and the answers are beyond the tendency to name or evaluate. Schohaus (2012/1932), almost 100 years ago, expertly grounded this inquiry in the aims of schooling and set forth an agenda for autonomy, connectedness, authenticity, and transcendence (Polizzi & Frick, 2012; Starratt, 2005):

[T]here is but one thing to be done. The teachers [and administrators] must carry out their work as though the children were of more importance to them than the educational system, and that the development of *one* [emphasis added] personality were of greater value than the maintenance of the plans of the school organization. [M]oreover, everything must be based upon a deep love of humanity, in a faith in human nature, which will affirm all the manifold phenomena of youthful development, even when these seem to us as most strange or are exceedingly difficult for us, who look on, to understand. [Therefore] the chief requirement for the correct pedagogic treatment of individual pupils is the acquisition of a thorough understanding of the individual characters of the children themselves. [This] educational understanding means an active faith and a sharp-sighted love for all the good possibilities which as yet lie dormant within the character of children.

(pp. 75–76)

Let us bring the social, emotional, ethical, and academic together. Let us commit to the increased need to serve and meet the academic, social, and emotional needs of *all* students in more careful ways. There is more suffering and woe ahead of us in schools. We need to better equip ourselves to respond to, and mitigate against, the dark places.

References

Addis, A. (2019). Dignity, integrity, and the concept of a person. *ICL Journal, 13*(4), 323–372. https://doi.org/10.1515/icl-2019-0015

Agosta, L. (2020, August 7). *Empathy and Hermeneutics.* https://louagosta.com/category/hermeneutic-circle/

Baker, D. P. (2014). *The schooled society: The educational transformation of global culture.* Stanford University Press.

Baker, D.P., Leon, J., Smith Greenaway, E.G., Collins, J. and Movit, M. (2011), The education effect on population health: A reassessment. *Population and Development Review*, 37: 307–332. https://doi.org/10.1111/j.1728-4457.2011.00412.x

Bohte, J., & Meier, K. J. (2002). Goal displacement: Assessing the motivation for organizational cheating. *Public Administration Review, 60*(2), 173–182. https://doi.org/10.1111/0033-3352.00075

Cassell, E. J. (1999). Diagnosing suffering: a perspective. *Annals of Internal Medicine, 131*(7).

Chapman, C. R., & Gavrin, J. (1993). Suffering and its relationship to pain. *Journal of Palliative Care, 9*(2), 5–13. https://doi.org/10.1177/082585979300900202

Chödrön, P. (1997). *When things fall apart: Heart advice for difficult times.* Shambhala Publications.

Corey, G. (2011). *Theory and practice of counseling and psychotherapy.* Brooks/Cole Cengage Learning.

Cox, G. (2021, August/September). *Kierkegaard: Young free and anxious.* Philosophy Now. https://philosophynow.org/issues/145

Crawford, M. B. (2006). Shop class as soulcraft. *The New Atlantis, 13,* 7–24.

Crowell, S. (2020). "Existentialism," *The Stanford Encyclopedia of Philosophy* (Summer 2020 Edition), E. N. Zalta (Ed.), URL = https://plato.stanford.edu/archives/sum2020/entries/existentialism/

Day, J. K., Fish, J. N., Grossman, A. H., & Russell, S. T. (2020). Gay-straight alliances, inclusive policy, and school climate: LGBTQ youths' experiences of social support and bullying. *Journal of Research on Adolescence, 30*(Suppl 2), 418–430. https://doi.org/10.1111/jora.12487

Davies, J. (2012) *The importance of suffering: the value and meaning of emotional discontent.* Routledge.

Drescher, K. D., Foy, D. W., Kelly, C., Leshner, A., Schutz, K., & Litz, B. (2011). An exploration of the viability and usefulness of the construct of moral injury in war veterans. *Traumatology, 17*(1), 8–13. https://doi.org/10.1177/1534765610395615

Driver, M. (2007). Meaning and suffering in organizations. *Journal of Organizational Change Management, 20*(5), 611–632. https://doi.org/10.1108/09534810710779063

Eizadirad, A., & Sider, S. (2021). Pedagogy of visibilizing pain and suffering: A commentary on the special issue. *Diaspora, Indigenous, and Minority Education, 15*(4), 221–223.

Evans, J., Rich, R., Allwood, R., Davies, B., (2008). Body Pedagogies, P/policy, health and gender, British Educational Research Journal. *34*:(3), 387–407. DOI 10.1080/01411920802042812

Faircloth, S. (2021). Ensuring American Indian students receive an equitable, just and appropriate education: A matter of personal and professional concern. *American Educator, 44*(4) 28–29, 32–34, 40.

Floyd, S. (2010). Education *as* soulcraft: Exemplary intellectual practice and the cardinal virtues. *Studies in Christian Ethics, 23*(3), 249–266.

Frank, A. (1992). The pedagogy of suffering: moral dimensions of psychological therapy and research with the ill. *Theory and Psychology*, 2(4) 467–485

Freud, S. (1930). *Civilization and its discontents.* Hogarth.

Frick, W. C. & Covaleskie, J. F. (2014). Preparation for integrity. In C. Branson & S. J. Gross (Eds.), *Handbook of ethical educational leadership* (pp. 386–404). Routledge.

Frick, W. C., Faircloth, S. C., & Little, K. S. (2013). Responding to the collective and individual "best interests of students": Revisiting the tension between administrative practice and ethical imperatives in special education leadership. *Educational Administration Quarterly, 49*(2), 207–242. https://doi.org/10.1177/0013161X12463230

Fullan, M. (2019, April 22). Why pedagogy and politics must partner. *Education Week.*

Glucksman, M.L. (2020). The therapeutic relationship reexamined: clinical and neurobiological aspects of empathic attunement. *Psychodynamic Psychiatry* 2020 48:4, 392–406.

Graves, R. L., & Swain S. S. (2016). Soulcraft in the classroom. In J. Buley, D. Buley, & R. Collister (Eds.), *The art of noticing deeply: Commentaries on teaching, learning, and mindfulness.* Cambridge Scholars Publishing.

Hanushek, E. A., Jamison, D. T., Jamison, E. A., & Woessmann, L. (2022). Education and economic growth: It's not just going to school but learning something while there that matters. *Education Next 22*(1), https://www.educationnext.org/education-and-economic-growth/

Harber, C. (2004). *Schooling as violence: how schools harm pupils and societies.* Routledge. https://doi.org/10.4324/9780203488423

Heifetz, R., & Laurie, D. L. (2001). The work of leadership. *Harvard Business Review, 79*(11), 131–141.

van Hooft S. (2000). The Suffering Body. *Health*, 4(2):179–195. https://doi.org/10.1177/136345930000400203

Kanov, J. M., Maitlis, S., Worline, M. C., Dutton, J. E., Frost, P. J., & Lilius, J. M. (2004). Compassion in organizational life. *American Behavioral Scientist, 47*(6), 808–827. https://doi.org/10.1177/0002764203260211

Kierkegaard, S. (1980). *The Concept of Anxiety: a simple psychologically orienting deliberation on the dogmatic issue of hereditary sin.* (Ed. & Trans. Thomte, R. with Anderson, A.). Princeton University Press.

Litz, B. T., Stein, N., Delaney, E., Lebowitz, L., Nash, W. P., Silva, C., & Maguen, S. (2009). Moral injury and moral repair in war veterans: A preliminary model and intervention strategy. *Clinical Psychology Review, 29*(8), 695–706. https://doi.org/10.1016/j.cpr.2009.07.003

Moffett, J. (2006). Soul school. In R. Foehr & S. Schiller (Eds.), *The spiritual side of writing: Releasing the learner's whole potential* (pp. 5–14). Heinemann.

Moreno, M. L., Rodrigo, M. M. T., Torres, J. M. R., Gaspar, T. J., & Agapito, J. L. (2021). *Cura personalis*: Institutionalizing compassion during emergency remote teaching. In M. M. T. Rodrigo, et al. (Eds.). *Proceedings of the 29th International Conference on Computers in Education.* Asia-Pacific Society for Computers in Education. https://icce2021.apsce.net/

Muñoz-Plaza, C., Quinn, S. C., & Rounds, K. A. (2002). Lesbian, gay, bisexual and transgender students: Perceived social support in the high school environment. *The High School Journal, 85*(4), 52–63. http://www.jstor.org/stable/40364353

Nussbaum, M. C. (2001). *Upheavals of thought: The intelligence of emotions* Cambridge University Press.

Otte, K. A. (2015). *Exploring themes of moral injury and resilience among women in a transitional living center.* [Unpublished doctoral dissertation] https://digitalcommons.pepperdine.edu/etd/612/

Polizzi, J. A., & Frick, W. C. (2012). Transformative preparation and professional development: authentic reflective practice for school leadership. *Teaching and Learning, 26*(1), 20–34 https://link.gale.com/apps/doc/A284937773/AONE?u=anon~f940fdea&sid=googleScholar&xid=7842f434

Polizzi, J. A., & Ronan, D. (2020). Contemplation for educators: theoretical, ethical and practical dimensions drawn from the Catholic intellectual tradition. *Values and Ethics in Educational Administration, 15*(2), PAGES

Santoro, D. A. (2011). Good teaching in difficult times: Demoralization in the pursuit of good work. *American Journal of Education, 118*(1), 1–23.

Schohaus, W. (2012/1932). The dark places of education: with a collection of 78 reports of school experiences. (M. Chadwick , Trans.). Routledge.

Seppälä, E. Simon-Thomas, S. Brown, M.C. Worline, C.D. Cameron and J.R. Doty (Eds.). The oxford handbook of compassion science (pp. 205–217). Oxford. DOI: 10.1093/oxfordhb/9780190464684.013.16

Spillane, J. P., & Lowenhaupt, R. (2019). *Navigating the principalship: Key insights for new and aspiring school leaders.* ASCD.

Starrat, J. (2005). *Building an ethical school: A practical response to the moral crisis in schools.* Routledge Falmer.

Starratt, R. J. (1991). Building an ethical school: A theory for practice in educational leadership. *Educational Administration Quarterly, 27*(2), 185–202. https://doi.org/10.1177/0013161X91027002005

Stiegler, JR, Molde, H, Schanche, E. (2018). Does an emotion-focused two-chair dialogue add to the therapeutic effect of the empathic attunement to affect? *Clinical Psychology & Psychotherapy.* 25: e86– e95. https://doi.org/10.1002/cpp.2144

Tuana, N. (2007). Conceptualizing moral literacy, *Journal of Educational Administration,* *45*(4), 364–378. https://doi.org/10.1108/09578230710762409

Tyack, D., & Cuban, L. (1995). *Tinkering toward utopia: A century of public school reform.* Harvard University Press.

VanderWeele T. J. (2019). Suffering and response: Directions in empirical research. *Social science & medicine,* 1982 (224), 58–66. https://doi.org/10.1016/j.socscimed.2019.01.041

VanHooft, S. (1998). The meanings of suffering. Hastings Center Report 28 5 (pp. 13–19).

Winnicott, D. W. (1971). *Playing and Reality.* Penguin Books.

Wolke, D., & Lereya S. T. (2015). Long-term effects of bullying. *Archives of Disease in Childhood; 100,* 879–885.

Weisz, E. & Zaki, J. (2017). Empathy-Building Interventions: A Review of Existing Work and Suggestions for Future Directions. In E.M.

Worsfold, V. L. (1980). Students' rights: Education in the just society. In W. Aiken & H. LaFollette (Eds.), *Whose child? Children's rights, parental authority, and state power* (pp. 254–273). Littlefield, Adams & Co.

Zimbardo, P., Seppälä, E., & Franco, Z. (2017). Heroism: social transformation through compassion in action. In E. M. Seppälä, E. Simon-Thomas, S.L. Brown, M.C. Worline, C. Daryl Cameron & J. R. Doty (Eds.) *The Oxford handbook of compassion science.* (pp. 487–493). Oxford University Press. https://doi.org/10.1093/oxfordhb/9780190464684.013.34

7 Concluding Thoughts on Suffering in School [Epilogue]

Shining a light on lament, sorrow, and suffering in school and coming to understand its place is likely the fruit of our labor. Words are inadequate to express the profound sorrow and distress felt throughout this study. Within our own grappling though, participants and their reports teach us something we hope is evident in the work: an inherent dignity at the center of our collective humanity. No words can take away the suffering our participants experienced, but their lesson is taken seriously: the dignity of personhood does entail both very dark places and states of resplendent light (Moore, 2004).

What we reveal and recommend is hard for most schools. Just as in Schohaus's (2012/1932) era, so in ours. In general, schools are too large, classrooms are too large, and the sufferings of students are too large for the issues and challenges we lay out to be humanistically addressed in responsible ways as circumstances currently stand. But, for organized schooling and its profession there can be hopefulness hidden in the darkness (Holmes, 2021). To arrange and act, a visionary ideal necessarily resides at the center of our message and is presented as a challenge for everyone who cares about schooling. We have to do better under conditions that all too often disallow us to do so. That is why it is imperative to have a system of thought that can cultivate courage, empathy, and fortitude so that educators and others who care can remain with this scene of suffering in spite of its formidable nature (Johnston, 2013).

Understanding suffering in schools requires recognizing that the affective and creative parts of an aspiring and incumbent educators' formation will produce powerful emotions like rage, love, empathic pain, helplessness, disgust, power, and joy through encounters with the lives of students (Charon, 2017). The social and the emotional inhabit the affective and creative and are not directly addressed in the standards and codes guiding the profession. Elaborating on the place of emotion and its connection to full personhood, Charon (2017) explained that

> the capacity for such emotions, the volume of the emotional amphora of the self, is always widened, deepened, made more capacious, neverendingly, through our brushes with the beautiful, the horrible, and the imagined. And the emotions themselves, once befriended, unfurl in real relationships with real people, quite apart from one's aesthetic or intellectual life.

(p. 3)

DOI: 10.4324/9780429465499-7

Through *real* relationships with *real* people—the students and the adults who work with them—mutual respect of a shared vulnerability and joint understanding of suffering could be realized.

With respect to educational administrators in particular, leadership preparation programs adherent to the National Educational Leadership Preparation (NELP) Program Recognition Standards (in the United States) and other professional standards abroad focus on school vision and mission, curriculum alignments and audits, equity, ethics, family community engagement, and the legal, financial, and operational matters of schools, with scant attention paid to well-being. Yet, understanding suffering in schools speaks to the social and the emotional as a primary part of our humanity and correspondingly apparent in educational realms. A leader who understands suffering realizes that suffering is not the residual moment in the life of a student; it is a recognition of our shared human condition and our shared human dignity is reinforced when we acknowledge another's suffering (Frank, 1992; Milton, 2013) As such, ensuring a more fully humanistic orientation as a component of the education of our teachers and school leaders becomes paramount.

Plainly, it is a matter of finding concrete inspiration within an education for aspiring and incumbent teachers and leaders that can foster moral positions leading to modest and complex compassionate actions for alleviating the suffering of students and ultimately heal them. We advocate for educational leadership program curricula that incorporate the social, ethical, and emotional consisting of lessons that foster the development of compassion for others, the reduction of fear of receiving compassion from others, providing compassionate understanding to others, and showing compassion for oneself (Martin and Heineberg, 2017).

A new education is needed. Bear with us as we take a brief journey through time. In 1932 (the same year Schohaus's *The Dark Places of Education* was published in English) the New Era Education and the New Education Fellowship met in Nice, France, where they presented their updated statement of principles which declared:

> In twenty years education might transform the social order and establish a spirit of co-operation capable of finding solutions for the problems of our time....It is only an education which realizes a change of attitude to children ... that can inaugurate an era free from the ruinous rivalries, the prejudices, anxieties and distress characteristic of our present chaotic insecure civilization.

> (Stewart and McCann, 1968, p. 226)

The call proved prescient. Twenty years on from 1932, brings us to December 9, 1952, when *Brown v. Board of Education* was first argued, and subsequently two years later, legally changed the social order. Today, in 2022, as in 1932, we are faced with a similar depression, although not necessarily one of global economic proportions, but one sadly of human proportions:

> In a meta-analysis of 29 studies including 80,879 youth globally, the pooled prevalence estimates of clinically elevated child and adolescent depression and anxiety were 25.2% and 20.5%, respectively. The prevalence of depression and anxiety symptoms during COVID-19 have doubled, compared with prepandemic estimates, and moderator analyses revealed that prevalence rates were higher when collected later in the pandemic, in older adolescents, and in girls. Meaning [that] the global estimates of child and adolescent mental illness observed in the first year of the COVID-19 pandemic in this study indicate that the prevalence has significantly increased, remains high, and therefore warrants attention for mental health recovery planning.
>
> (Racine et al., 2021, pp. 1142–1143)

The sheer number of suffering students (1 in 4) is astounding and warrants the somber attention of educators, individuals, and organizations interested in a coordinated correction for a brighter future. Children and adolescents are suffering in schools *right now*. Time is of the essence as we do not have twenty years. We place responsibility for understanding and alleviating suffering in schools primarily with teachers and leaders to create, ensure, and sustain more careful, kind, equitable, and compassionate school policies, practices, and cultures. Schohaus's words are most relevant to conclude with:

> Let us rejoice to be the pioneers of the schools of the future, where everything possible will be done lovingly to confirm young people in all their impulses for life and development and to provide them a free, happy and a strong existence.
>
> (2012/1932, p. 337)

Sit finis operis, non finis quaerendi

References

Charon R. (2017). To see the suffering. *Academic Medicine: Journal of the Association of American Medical Colleges, 92*(12), 1668–1670. https://doi.org/10.1097/ACM.0000000000001989

Frank, A. W. (1992). The pedagogy of suffering: Moral dimensions of psychological therapy and research with the ill. *Theory & Psychology, 2*(4), 467–485. https://doi.org/10.1177/0959354392024004

Holmes, B. (2021, December 29). *The wisdom of darkness*. Center for Action and Contemplation. https://cac.org/the-wisdom-of-darkness-2021-12-29/?utm_source=cm&utm_medium=email&utm_campaign=dm&utm_content=summary

Johnston, N. E. (2013). Strengthening a praxis of suffering: Teaching-learning practices. *Nursing Science Quarterly, 26*(3), 230–235. https://doi.org/10.1177/0894318413489183

Martin, D. & Heineberg, Y. (2017). Social dominance and leadership: the mediational effects of compassion. In E.M. Seppälä, E. Simon-Thomas, S. L. Brown, M. C. Worline, C. Daryl Cameron & J. R. Doty (Eds.) *The Oxford handbook of compassion science.* (pp. 487–493). Oxford University Press. https://doi.org/10.1093/oxfordhb/9780190464684.013.35

Milton, C.L. (2013). Suffering. *Nursing Science Quarterly, 26(3),* 226-228.

Moore, T. (2004). *Dark nights of the soul: A guide for finding your way through life's ordeals.* Penguin Random House.

Racine N., McArthur B.A., Cooke J. E., Eirich R., Zhu J., & Madigan S. (2021) Global prevalence of depressive and anxiety symptoms in children and adolescents during COVID-19: A Meta-analysis. *JAMA Pediatr.,* *175*(11), 1142–1150. doi:10.1001/jamapediatrics.2021.2482

Schohaus, W. (2012/1932). *The dark places of education* (M. Chadwick, Trans.) Routledge.

Stewart, W. A. C., & McCann, W. P. (1968). *The Educational Innovators: Volume II: Progressive Schools 1881–1967.* Palgrave Macmillan UK.

Index

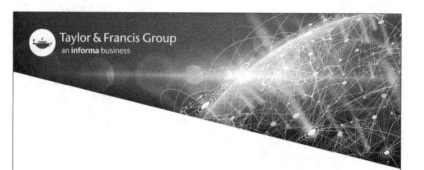

CPSIA information can be obtained
at www.ICGtesting.com
Printed in the USA
LVHW081441060922
727702LV00005B/226